THE WEAPONS OF
MYSTERY

JOSEPH HOCKING

1st WORLD
LIBRARY
Literary Society

The Weapons of Mystery

Joseph Hocking

© 1st World Library, 2007
PO Box 2211
Fairfield, IA 52556
www.1stworldlibrary.com
First Edition

LCCN: 2007930805

Softcover ISBN: 978-1-4218-4844-0
Hardcover ISBN: 978-1-4218-4747-4
eBook ISBN: 978-1-4218-4941-6

Purchase *"The Weapons of Mystery"*
as a traditional bound book at:
www.1stWorldLibrary.com/purchase.asp?ISBN=978-1-4218-4844-0

1st World Library is a literary, educational organization
dedicated to:

- Creating a free internet library of downloadable ebooks

- Hosting writing competitions and offering book publishing
scholarships.

Interested in more 1st World Library books? contact:
literacy@1stworldlibrary.com
Check us out at: www.1stworldlibrary.com

1ˢᵗ World Library Literary Society

Giving Back to the World

"If you want to work on the core problem, it's early school literacy."

- James Barksdale, former CEO of Netscape

"No skill is more crucial to the future of a child, or to a democratic and prosperous society, than literacy."

- Los Angeles Times

"Literacy... means far more than learning how to read and write... The aim is to transmit... knowledge and promote social participation."

- UNESCO

"Literacy is not a luxury, it is a right and a responsibility. If our world is to meet the challenges of the twenty-first century we must harness the energy and creativity of all our citizens."

- President Bill Clinton

"Parents should be encouraged to read to their children, and teachers should be equipped with all available techniques for teaching literacy, so the varying needs and capacities of individual kids can be taken into account."

- Hugh Mackay

CONTENTS

CHAPTER I

INTRODUCES THE WRITER AND OTHERS

My story begins on the morning of December 18, 18—, while sitting at breakfast. Let it be understood before we go further that I was a bachelor living in lodgings. I had been left an orphan just before I came of age, and was thus cast upon the world at a time when it is extremely dangerous for young men to be alone. Especially was it so in my case, owing to the fact that at twenty-one I inherited a considerable fortune. One thing saved me from ruin, viz. a passionate love for literature, which led me to make it my profession. I had at the time of my story been following the bent of my inclinations for two years with a fair amount of success, and was regarded by those who knew me as a lucky fellow. That is all I think I need say concerning myself prior to the time when my story opens, except to tell my name; but that will drop out very soon. I had not made very great inroads into the omelette my landlady had prepared for me when I heard the postman's knock, and soon after a servant entered with a letter. One only. I had expected at least half-a-dozen, but only one lay on the tray before me.

"Are you sure this is all, Jane?" I asked.

"Quite sure, sir," said Jane, smiling, and then with a curtsey she took her leave.

The envelope was addressed in a bold hand-writing to—

Justin M. Blake, Esq.,
Gower Street,
London, W.

"Surely I know the writing," I mused, and then began to look at the postmarks as if a letter were something of very uncommon occurrence. I could make nothing of the illegible smear in the corner, however, and so opened it, and read as follows:—

Dear old Justin Martyr,

I suppose you have about forgotten your old schoolfellow, Tom Temple, and it's natural you should; but he has not forgotten you. You see, you have risen to fame, and I have remained in obscurity. Ah well, such is the fate of that community called 'country gentlemen.' But this is not what I want to write about, and I am going straight to the real object of this letter.

We—that is, mother, the girls, and myself—are contemplating a real jolly Christmas. We are inviting a few friends to spend Christmas and New Year with us, and we wish you to make one of the number. Will you come and spend a fortnight or so at Temple Hall? Of course it is rather quiet here, but we are going to do our best to make it more lively than usual. The weather looks frosty, and that promises skating. We have a few good horses, so that we can have some rides across the country. There is also plenty of shooting, hunting, etc., etc. Altogether, if you will come and help us; we can promise a fairly good bill of fare. What do you say? You must excuse me for writing in this unconventional strain, but I can't write otherwise to my old schoolfellow.

We shall all be really disappointed if you say 'no,' so write at once and tell us you will come, also when we may expect you. All the news when we meet.

Your sincere friend,

Tom Temple.

P.S.—I might say that most of the guests will arrive on Christmas Eve.

"Just the very thing," I exclaimed. "I had been wondering what to do and where to go this Christmas time, and this invitation comes in splendidly."

Tom Temple lived in Yorkshire, at a fine old country house some distance from the metropolis of that county, and was a really good fellow. As for his mother and sisters, I knew but little about them, but I judged from the letters his mother wrote him when at school, that she must be a true, kind-hearted, motherly woman.

I accordingly turned to my desk, wrote to Tom, telling him to expect me on the 24th inst., and then, without finishing my breakfast, endeavoured to go on with my work. It was very difficult, however. My thoughts were ever running away to Yorkshire, and on the pleasant time I hoped to spend. Between the lines on my paper I was ever seeing the old baronial hall that was Tom Temple's home, and the people who had been invited to spend the festive season there. Presently I began to chide myself for my foolishness. Why should the thoughts of a Christmas holiday so unfit me, a staid old bachelor of thirty, for my usual work? Nevertheless it did, so I put on my overcoat, and went away in the direction of Hyde Park in order, if possible, to dispel my fancies. I did dispel them, and shortly afterwards returned to my lodgings, and did a good morning's work.

Nothing of importance happened between the 18th and the 24th, and early in the afternoon of the latter date I found my way to St. Pancras Station, and booked for the station nearest Tom Temple's home. Although it was Christmas Eve, I found an empty first-class carriage, and soon comfortably ensconced myself therein. I don't know why, but we English people generally try to get an empty carriage, and feel annoyed when some one comes in to share our possession. I, like the rest of my countrymen are apt to do in such a case, began to hope I might retain the entire use of the carriage, at least to Leeds, when the door opened, and a porter brought a number of wraps and shawls, evidently the property of a lady.

"Bother it!" I mentally exclaimed, "and so I suppose I am to have some fidgety old women for my travelling companions."

The reader will imagine from this that I was not a lady's man. At any rate, such was the case. I had lived my thirty years without ever being in love; indeed, I had from principle avoided the society of ladies, that is, when they were of the flirtable or marriageable kind.

No sooner had the porter laid the articles mentioned on a corner seat, the one farthest away from me, than their owner entered, and my irritation vanished. It was a young lady under the ordinary size, and, from what I could see of her, possessed of more than ordinary beauty. Her skin was dark and clear, her eyes very dark, her mouth pleasant yet decided, her chin square and determined. This latter feature would in the eyes of many destroy her pretensions to beauty, but I, who liked persons with a will of their own, admired the firm resoluteness the feature indicated.

She took no notice of me, but quietly arranged her belongings as if she were accustomed to take care of herself. She had only just sat down, when she was followed by another lady, who appeared, from the sign of recognition that passed between them, an acquaintance.

Evidently, however, the younger lady was not delighted at the advent of the elder. A look of annoyance swept across her face, as if she could have very comfortably excused her presence. I did not wonder at it. This second comer was a woman of about fifty-five years of age. She had yellow wrinkled skin, a square upright forehead, shaggy grey eyebrows, beneath which, in two cavernous sockets, were two black beady-looking eyes. Her mouth was large and coarse, and, to make that feature still more objectionable, two large teeth, like two fangs, stuck out at a considerable angle from her upper jaw and rested on the lower lip. Altogether the face was repulsive. Added to this, she was tall and bony, and would have passed anywhere for one of the witches of olden time.

"I have altered my mind, Gertrude, and am going with you." This was said in a harsh, thick voice.

"I see you are here, Miss Staggles," said the younger lady very coolly.

"I did not intend coming at first, but your aunt, poor silly thing, said you would not take your maid with you, and so I thought it would be a sin for a young girl like you to travel alone to Yorkshire on a day like this."

"Yorkshire?" I thought. "Is that old woman to be in this

carriage with me for five or six long hours? I'll get out."

I was too late; at that moment the guard's whistle blew, and the train moved slowly out of the station. At all events, I had to remain until the train stopped, so I composed myself as well as I could, and resolved to make the best of it. Neither of them paid the slightest attention to me. The elder lady sat bolt upright opposite the younger, and began to harangue her.

"Don't you know it was very foolish of you to think of coming alone?"

"No," said the younger lady; "I'm tired of having a maid dogging my every footstep, as if I were a child and unable to do for myself."

"Nevertheless, Gertrude, you should have brought her; no young lady should travel alone. However, you will have a chaperon, so the deficiency will be more than remedied;" and there was grim satisfaction in the woman's voice.

There was no satisfaction in the young lady's face, however, and she turned with what I thought an angry look towards the scrawny duenna, who had claimed guardianship over her, and said—

"But, Miss Staggles, you are in a false position. You have received no invitation."

"No, I have not; but your aunt had one, poor silly creature, and so, for duty's sake, I am breaking the rules of etiquette. Those fine people you are about to visit did not think it worth their while to invite your aunt's late husband's step-sister—perhaps because she is poor; but she has a soul above formalities, and so determined to come and take care of her niece."

The young lady made no reply.

"You will be thankful, Gertrude Forrest, some day that I do care for you," Miss Staggles continued, "although I never expect to get any reward for my kindness."

By this time the train was going rapidly, and so loud was the roar it made that I heard only the growling of Miss Staggles' voice without distinguishing any words. Indeed, I was very glad I could not. It was by no means pleasant to have to sit and listen to her hoarse voice, so I pulled down the laps of my travelling cap over my ears and, closing my eyes, began to think who Gertrude Forrest was, and where she was going.

I did not change carriages as I intended. Miss Staggles got tired after awhile, and so there was relief in that quarter, while my seat was most comfortable, and I did not want to be disturbed. Hour after hour passed by, until night came on; then the wind blew colder, and I began to wonder how soon the journey would end, when the collector came to take all the tickets from the Leeds passengers. Shortly after we arrived at the Midland station, for which I was truly thankful. I did not wait there long; a train stood at another platform, which stopped at a station some two miles from Tom Temple's home. By this time there was every evidence of the holiday season. The train was crowded, and I was glad to get in at all, unmindful of comfort.

What had become of my two travelling companions I was not aware, but concluded that they would be staying at Leeds, as they had given up their tickets at the collecting station. I cannot but admit, however, that I was somewhat anxious as to the destination of Gertrude Forrest, for certainly she had made an impression upon me I was not likely to forget. Still I gave up the idea of ever seeing her again, and tried to think of the visit I was about to pay.

Arrived at the station, I saw Tom Temple, who gave me a hearty welcome, after which he said, "Justin, my boy, do you want to be introduced to some ladies at present?"

"A thousand times no," I replied. "Let's wait till we get to Temple Hall."

"Then, in that case, you will have to go home in a cab. I retained one for you, knowing your dislike to the fair sex; for, of course, they will have to go in the carriage, and I must go with them. Stay, though. I'll go and speak to them, and get them all safe in the carriage, and then, as there will be barely room for me, I'll come back and ride home with you."

He rushed away as he spoke, and in a few minutes came back again. "I am sorry those ladies had to be made rather uncomfortable, but guests have been arriving all the day, and thus things are a bit upset. There are five people in yon carriage; three came from the north, and two from the south. The northern train has been in nearly half-an-hour, so the three had to wait for the two. Well, I think I've made them comfortable, so I don't mind so much."

"You're a capital host, Tom," I said.

"Am I, Justin? Well, I hope I am to you, for I have been really longing for you to come, and I want you to have a jolly time."

"I'm sure I shall," I replied.

"Well, I hope so; only you don't care for ladies' society, and I'm afraid I shall have to be away from you a good bit."

"Naturally you will, old fellow. You see, you are master of the hall, and will have to look after the comfort of all the guests."

"Oh, as to that, mother will do all that's necessary; but I— that is—" and Tom stopped.

"Any particular guest, Tom?" I asked.

"Yes, there is, Justin. I don't mind telling you, but I'm in love, and I want to settle the matter this Christmas. She's an angel of a girl, and I'm in hopes that—Well, I don't believe she hates me."

"Good, Tom. And her name?"

"Her name," said Tom slowly, "is Edith Gray."

I gave a sigh of relief. I could not help it—why I could not tell; and yet I trembled lest he should mention another name.

We reached Temple Hall in due time, where I was kindly welcomed by Mrs. Temple and her two daughters. The former was just the kind of lady I had pictured her, while the daughters gave promise of following in the footsteps of their kind-hearted mother.

Tom took me to my room, and then, looking at his watch, said, "Make haste, old fellow. Dinner has been postponed on account of you late arrivals, but it will be ready in half-an-hour."

I was not long over my toilet, and soon after hearing the first dinner bell I wended my way to the drawing-room, wondering who and what kind of people I should meet, but was not prepared for the surprises that awaited me.

CHAPTER II

CHRISTMAS EVE

Just before I reached the drawing-room door, Mrs. Temple came up and took me by the arm.

"We are all going to be very unceremonious, Mr. Blake," she said, "and I shall expect my son's friend to make himself perfectly at home."

I thanked her heartily, for I began to feel a little strange.

We entered the drawing-room together, where I found a number of people had gathered. They were mostly young, although I saw one or two ancient-looking dames, who, I supposed, had come to take care of their daughters.

"I am going to introduce you to everybody," continued the old lady, "for this is to be a family gathering, and we must all know each other. I know I may not be acting according to the present usages of society, but that does not trouble me a little bit."

Accordingly, with the utmost good taste, she introduced me to a number of the people who had been invited.

Joseph Hocking

I need make no special mention of most of them. Some of the young ladies simpered, others were frank, some were fairly good looking, while others were otherwise, and that is about all that could be said. None had sufficient individuality to make a distinct impression upon me. The young men were about on a par with the young ladies. Some lisped and were affected, some were natural and manly; and I began to think that, as far as the people were concerned, the Christmas gathering would be a somewhat tame affair.

This thought had scarcely entered my mind when two men entered the room, who were certainly not of the ordinary type, and will need a few words of description; for both were destined, as my story will show, to have considerable influence over my life.

I will try to describe the more striking of the two first.

He was a young man. Not more than thirty-five. He was fairly tall, well built, and had evidently enjoyed the education and advantages of a man of wealth. His hair was black as the raven's wings, and was brushed in a heavy mass horizontally across his forehead. His eyes were of a colour that did not accord with his black hair and swarthy complexion. They were of an extremely light grey, and were tinted with a kind of green. They were placed very close together, and, the bridge of the nose being narrow, they appeared sometimes as if only one eye looked upon you. The mouth was well cut, the lips rather thin, which often parted, revealing a set of pearly white teeth. There was something positively fascinating about the mouth, and yet it betrayed malignity—cruelty. He was perfectly self-possessed, stood straight, and had a soldier-like bearing. I instinctively felt that this was a man of power, one who would endeavour to make his will law. His movements were perfectly graceful, and from the flutter among the young ladies when he entered, I judged he had already spent some little time with them, and made no slight impression.

His companion was much smaller, and even darker than he was. His every feature indicated that he was not an Englishman. With small wiry limbs, black, restless, furtive eyes, rusty black hair, and a somewhat unhealthy colour in his face, he formed a great contrast to the man I have just tried to describe. I did not like him. He seemed to carry a hundred secrets around with him, and each one a deadly weapon he would some day use against any who might offend him. He, too, gave you the idea of power, but it was the power of a subordinate.

Instinctively I felt that I should have more to do with these men than with the rest of the company present.

Although I have used a page of good paper in describing them, I was only a very few seconds in seeing and realizing what I have written.

Both walked up to us, and both smiled on Mrs. Temple, whereupon she introduced them. The first had a peculiar name; at least, so it seemed to me.

"Mr. Herod Voltaire—Mr. Justin Blake," she said; and instantly we were looking into each other's eyes, I feeling a strange kind of shiver pass through me.

The name of the smaller man was simply that of an Egyptian, "Aba Wady Kaffar." The guests called him Mr. Kaffar, and thus made it as much English as possible.

Scarcely had the formalities of introduction been gone through between the Egyptian and myself, when my eyes were drawn to the door, which was again opening. Do what I would I could not repress a start, for, to my surprise, I saw my travelling companions enter with Miss Temple—Gertrude Forrest looking more charming and more beautiful than ever, and beside her Miss Staggles, tall, gaunt, and more forbidding than when in the railway carriage.

It is no use denying the fact, for my secret must sooner or later drop out. My heart began to throb wildly, while my brain seemed on fire. I began to picture myself in conversation with her, and becoming acquainted with her, when I accidentally looked at Herod Voltaire. His eyes were fixed on Miss Forrest, as if held by a magnet, and I fancied I saw a faint colour tinge his cheek.

What I am now going to write may appear foolish and unreal, especially when you remember that I was thirty years of age, but the moment I saw his ardent, admiring gaze, I felt madly jealous.

The second dinner bell rang, and so, mechanically offering my arm to a lady who had, I thought, been neglected on account of her plain looks, I followed the guests to the dining-room.

Nothing happened there worth recording. We had an old-fashioned English dinner, and that is about all I can remember, except that the table looked exceedingly nice. I don't think there was much talking; evidently the guests were as yet strangers to each other, and were only gradually wearing away the restraint that naturally existed. I could not see Miss Gertrude Forrest, for she was sitting on my side of the table, but I could see the peculiar eyes of Herod Voltaire constantly looking at some one nearly opposite him, while he scarcely touched the various dishes that were placed on the table.

Presently dinner came to an end. The ladies retired to the drawing-room, while the gentlemen prepared to sit over their wine. Being an abstainer, I asked leave to retire with the ladies. I did this for two reasons besides my principles of abstinence. First, I thought the custom a foolish one, as well as being harmful; and, second, I hoped by entering the drawing-room early, I might have a chance to speak to Miss Forrest.

I did not leave alone. Two young Englishmen also declared themselves to be abstainers, and wanted to go with me, while Herod Voltaire likewise asked leave to abide by the rules he had ever followed in the countries in which he had lived.

Of course there was some laughing demur among those who enjoyed their after-dinner wine, but we followed the bent of our inclination, and found our way to the drawing-room.

Evidently the ladies were not sorry to see us, for a look of pleasure and surprise greeted us, and soon the conversation became general. Presently, however, our attention was by degrees drawn to that part of the room where Herod Voltaire sat, and I heard him speaking fluently and smoothly on some subject he was discussing with a young lady.

"Yes, Miss Emery," he said, "I think European education is poor, is one-sided. Take, for example, the ordinary English education, and what does it amount to? Arithmetic, and sometimes a little mathematics, reading, writing, French, sometimes German, and of course music and dancing. Nearly all are educated in one groove, until there is in the English mind an amount of sameness that becomes monotonous."

"You are speaking of the education of ladies, Mr. Voltaire?" said Miss Emery.

"Yes, more particularly, although there is but little more variation among the men. Take your University degrees— your Cambridge and Oxford Master of Arts, for example; what a poor affair it is! I have been looking over the subjects of examination, and what are they? A couple of languages, the literature of two or three countries, mathematics, and something else which I have forgotten now."

"You are scarcely correct, sir," said one of the young men who came in with me. "I happen to have passed through Cambridge, and have taken the degree you mention. I found it stiff enough."

"Not so stiff, when it can be taken at your age," replied Voltaire. "But, admitting what you say, you are all cast in the same mould. You study the same subjects, and thus what one of you knows, all know."

"And what may be your ideas concerning education?" said Miss Forrest.

Herod Voltaire turned and looked admiringly on her, and I saw that a blush tinged both their cheeks.

"My ideas are such as would not find much favour in ordinary English circles," he said smilingly. "But I should do away with much of the nonsense of ordinary English education, and deal with the more occult sciences."

"Pardon me, but I do not quite understand you."

"I will endeavour to make my meaning plain. There are subjects relating to the human body, mind, and soul, which cannot be said to have been really studied at all, except by some recluse here and there, who is generally considered mad. You deal with the things which are seen, but think not of the great unsolved spiritual problems of life. For example, the effect of mind upon mind, animal magnetism, mesmerism, biology, and kindred subjects are unknown to you. The secrets of mind and spirit are left unnoticed by you Western people. You seek not to solve the occult truths which exist in the spirit of all men. You shudder at the problem of what you call death, and fancy nothing can be known of the spirit which leaves the world in which you live; whereas there is no such thing as death. The spirits of the so-called dead are living forces all around us, who can tell their condition to those who understand some of the secrets of spiritualism. Nay, more than that. There are occult laws of the soul which, if understood by some powerful mind, can be made to explain some of the deepest mysteries of the universe. For example, a man versed in the secrets of the spirit life can cause the soul of any human being to leave its clay tenement, and go to the world of spirits, and learn its secrets; and by the powers of his soul life, which can be a thousand times strengthened by means of a knowledge of the forces at the command of all, he can summon it back to the body again. Of course I can only hint at these things here, as only the initiated can understand these secret laws; but these are the things I would have studied, and thus lift the life of man beyond his poor material surroundings." By this time the drawing-room was pretty well full. Nearly all the men had left their wine, and all were listening intently to what Voltaire was saying.

"You have lived in the East?" said Miss Forrest, evidently fascinated by the strange talk.

"For the last ten years. I spent a year in Cairo, two more up by the banks of the Nile, among the ruins of ancient cities, where, in spite of the degradation that exists, there is still to be found those who have some of the wisdom of past ages. Four years did I live in India among the sages who hold fast to the teaching of Buddha. The three remaining years I have spent in Arabia, Syria, and Chaldea."

"And do you mean to say that what you have mentioned exists in reality?" said Miss Forrest.

"I have only hinted at what really exists. I could record to you facts that are strange, beyond the imagination of Dumas; so wonderful, that afterwards you could believe the stories told by your most renowned satirist, Dean Swift."

"Favour us with one," I suggested.

Voltaire looked at me with his green-tinted eyes, as if he would read my innermost thoughts. Evidently his impression of me was not favourable, for a cynical smile curled his lips, and his eyes gleamed with a steely glitter. "One has to choose times, occasions, and proper circumstances, in order to tell such facts," he said. "I never speak of a sacred thing jestingly."

We were all silent. This man had become the centre of attraction. Both men and women hung upon his every word. I looked around the room and I saw a strange interest manifested, except in the face of the Egyptian. Aba Wady Kaffar was looking at the ceiling as if calculating how many square feet there were.

"Perhaps you find it difficult to believe me," went on Voltaire. "The truth is, I am very unfortunate in many respects. My way of expressing my thoughts is perhaps distasteful to you. You see, I have lived so long in the East that I have lost much of my European training. Then, my name is unfortunate. Herod killed one of your Christian saints, while Voltaire was an infidel. You English people have strong prejudices, and thus my story would be injured by the narrator."

"Nay, Voltaire," said Tom Temple, "we are all friendly listeners here."

"My good host," said Voltaire, "I am sure you are a friendly listener, but I have been telling of Eastern knowledge. One aspect of that knowledge is that the learned can read the minds, the thoughts of those with whom they come into contact."

The ladies began to express an intense desire to hear a story of magic and mystery, and to assure him that his name was a delightful one.

"I trust I am not the disciple of either the men whose name I bear. Certainly I am susceptible to the influence of ladies"— and he smiled, thereby showing his white, shining teeth— "but I am a great admirer of honest men, whoever they may be, or whatever be their opinion. I am not a follower of Voltaire, although I admire his genius. He believed but little in the powers of the soul, or in the spirit world; I, on the other hand, believe it to be more real than the world in which we live."

"We are not altogether strangers to stories about spiritualism or mesmerism here," said Miss Forrest, "but the votaries of these so-called sciences have been and are such miserable specimens of mankind that educated people treat them with derision."

There was decision and energy in her voice. Evidently she was not one to be easily deceived or trifled with.

"Counterfeits prove reality," said Voltaire, looking searchingly at her; "besides, I seek to impose none of my stories on any one. I am not a professional spiritualist, psychologist, or biologist. I simply happen to have lived in countries where these matters are studied, and, as a consequence, have learned some of their mysteries. Seeing what I have seen, and hearing what I have heard, I beg to quote your greatest poet—

'There are more things in heaven and earth than are dreamt of in your philosophy.'

"Your quotation is apropos," she said in reply, "but it so happens that I have taken considerable interest in the matter about which you have been speaking, and after seeing various representations of these so-called occult sciences, and carefully examining them, I have come to the conclusion that they are only so many fairly clever juggling tricks, which have been attempts to deceive credulous people. Moreover, these have been so often exposed by cultured men, that they have no weight with people of intelligence."

His eyes gleamed savagely, but he smiled upon her, and said, "Perhaps I may have an opportunity of undeceiving you, some time in the near future."

"Meanwhile you will tell us an Eastern story," said one of the young ladies.

"Pardon me," replied Voltaire, "but tonight is Christmas Eve, and as my story might be regarded as heathenish, I will wait for some more favourable time, when your minds will not be influenced by the memories of the birth of the Christian religion. Besides, I know many of you are longing for other amusement than stories of the unseen."

As he spoke I saw his eyes travel towards Aba Wady Kaffar, and they exchanged glances; then he looked towards Miss

Forrest, and again a look of intelligence passed between him and the Egyptian.

Soon after Kaffar began to talk fluently to one of the Misses Temple, while several members of the party prepared for a charade. Then, when the attention of the guests was drawn towards those who displayed their powers at acting, I saw Voltaire rise and go out, and soon after he was followed by his friend.

Acting upon sudden impulse, which I think was caused by the remembrance of the meaning glances that passed between them after Voltaire had looked at Miss Forrest, I followed them out into the silent night. Somehow I felt that this fascinating man did not like me, while I was sure he had been deeply impressed by the woman who had that day travelled with me from London.

Joseph Hocking

CHAPTER III

CHRISTMAS MORNING

When I got out on the lawn, I accused myself of doing a very foolish thing. "Why," I thought, "should I follow these men? I know nothing against them. They have as much right here as I have, and surely two friends can leave the house and come out for a stroll without being watched?"

With this thought in my mind I turned to go back again, when I heard voices close by me. Evidently they were behind some large laurel bushes which hid them from my sight. I stopped again for an instant; but, knowing I had no right to listen to what might be private conversation, I started a second time for the house, when I heard the name of Gertrude Forrest, and then I seemed chained to the ground.

"You have inquired about her?" said a voice, which I recognized as belonging to Voltaire. The answer was in Arabic, and was spoken by Kaffar.

Five years prior to the time of which I am writing I had been engaged in a work that required a knowledge of the Arabic language, and although it cannot be said I had become anything like proficient in that tongue, I had been taught by an Arabian, and could enter into ordinary conversation. Thus

I understood the Egyptian's reply.

"With regard to Miss Forrest," he said, "I answer not in the language which every one here knows. Miss Forrest must be yours, and that for several reasons. She is a flower in herself. She is an orphan. She has a large fortune. She has absolute control over it. She has a fine house in England's capital. She has a large estate and a grand country mansion in the south of this country. Win her, Herod Voltaire, and you can be a little king, and I your prime minister. We heard much about her before we came; but we did not think to find such a queen. Win her, man, and our fortunes are made."

This was said quickly, and with all the fervour of an Eastern.

"Yes, Kaffar. It would be well if it could be done. To be an English gentleman, with an *entree* into the best English society, is what I have long longed for. It will not only satisfy my taste, but give me power, and power is what I must have. It is by good luck we are here, but neither of us have the means to pass as English aristocrats very long. As you say, something must be done, and, upon my honour, I have very nearly fallen in love with her. But she must be won, and won fairly. She is evidently strong and determined, and can be forced to do nothing."

"Nonsense," snarled the Egyptian. "Use all your seductive arts first, and if you fail to win her by those, trust me to weave such a chain of events as shall make her become Mrs. Voltaire."

Up to this point I listened attentively, and then a minute's silence on their part aroused me to myself. Was it right to stand listening thus? And yet a thousand things justified the act.

Joseph Hocking

They moved on from the spot where they had been standing, but I was too much stunned to follow them. At that moment I realized that I had given my heart to Gertrude Forrest, and that another man had designs concerning her.

This sudden falling into love may appear foolish, especially when it is remembered that I had passed the age of boyhood, and yet I have known several cases similar to my own. Anyhow, I, who had never loved before, loved now—loved, perhaps, foolishly; for I knew nothing of the lady I loved, and, of course, had not the slightest hope of her caring for me.

Thus it was with a throbbing heart that I stood there alone upon the lawn, with the knowledge of my new-found love just breaking upon me, and, more than that, I had every reason to fear that she was to be made the dupe of two clever villains.

I turned to follow them, but they were gone I knew not whither, and so I went back to the house determined that, if I could be nothing else, I would be Miss Forrest's protector.

I had been back in the drawing-room perhaps ten minutes, when Voltaire and Kaffar returned, and apparently entered with great zest into the festivities of the evening. There is no necessity that I should write of what took place during the remainder of Christmas Eve. It was held in good old English style, and to most, I am sure, it was very enjoyable. I got an opportunity of speaking to Miss Forrest, but only for a very short time; at the same time, I noticed that Voltaire took not the slightest notice of her.

When I awoke the following morning and looked out, I saw that the great Yorkshire hills were covered with snow, the air was bitingly cold, and the leaden sky promised us some real

Christmas weather.

I was soon dressed and ready to go down, but on looking at my watch I found I had an hour to spare before breakfast. Arrangements had been made for us to breakfast at ten, and thus be just in time for service at the little village church.

On my way down-stairs I saw Tom Temple, who told me to find my way to the library, where I should be able to pass the time pleasantly. I entered the room, an old-fashioned dark place lined on every side with books. I felt in no mood for looking at them just then, however, and so walked to a window and looked out on the snow-draped landscape that stretched away on every hand. It was a wondrous scene. The snow had fallen steadily all through the night, and no breath of wind had stirred the feathery flakes. Thus trees and bushes were laden with snow crystals, while the spotless white was relieved here and there by some shining evergreen leaves which peeped out amidst their snowy mantles. Ordinarily I should have been impressed by it. Now, however, I could not help thinking of other matters. One face was ever before me, and I constantly wondered whether she were in real danger from these strange men, and whether I should have any part in the labour of delivering her from them. As yet I could do nothing. I knew nothing wrong of them. They might be impostors, they might be penniless adventurers, but I could not prove it. Neither could I tell Miss Forrest what I had heard, while certainly Voltaire had as much right as I had to seek to win her affections.

These thoughts had scarcely passed through my mind when, hearing a sound behind me, I turned and saw Miss Forrest, who met me with a bright "Good-morning" and the compliments of the season. I blushed almost guiltily at the sound of her voice—I, who had for years declared that no woman could interest me enough to make my heart throb one whit the quicker.

"This is a pleasant surprise," I said, after responding to her greeting. "I quite expected to be alone for an hour at least. You see, we all remained up so late last night that it was to me a settled matter that none of you would appear until it was time to start for church."

"I hope I am not disturbing you in your morning's meditations, Mr. Blake," she replied; "I would have stayed in my room had I thought so."

"On the other hand, I am delighted to see you here. Whether you know it or not, I rode from London to Leeds with you yesterday, and I have thought ever since I should like to know you."

She looked straight at me as if she would read my thoughts, and then said pleasantly, "I was on the point of asking you whether such was not the case. I was not sure, because you had your travelling cap pulled over your face."

"How strange, though, that we were both bound for the same place!" I said.

"Yes, it does seem remarkable; and yet it is not so wonderful, after all. I am an old friend and schoolfellow of Emily Temple, while you, I am told, are an old friend and schoolfellow of her brother. Thus nothing is more natural than that we should be invited to such a gathering as this."

"Do you know any of the people who are here?" I asked.

"I have met nearly all the young ladies, but only two of the gentlemen—Mr. Voltaire and Mr. Kaffar. I saw them on the Continent."

"Indeed?" I said, while I have no doubt a dark look passed over my face.

"Do you not like them?" she asked.

"I do not know enough of either," I replied, "to give an answer reasonably, either in the affirmative or the negative. I think my failing is to form hasty judgments concerning people, which, of course, cannot be fair."

I said this rather stammeringly, while she watched me keenly.

"That means that you do not like them," she said.

"Are you quite justified in saying that?" I replied, scarcely knowing what else to say.

"Quite," she said. "You feel towards them just as I do. I was introduced to them in Berlin. Mr. Tom Temple had formed their acquaintance somehow, and seemed wonderfully fascinated by them. I scarcely spoke to them, however, as I left Germany the next day, and was rather surprised to see them here last night."

"Mr. Voltaire is a very fascinating man," I suggested.

"There can be no doubt about that," was her reply.

"And yet I fancy much of his high-flown talk about spiritualism was mere imagination."

"I was inclined to think so at first, but I have heard strange things about him. However, it is perhaps scarcely fair to talk about him thus."

All this time we had stood looking out of the window upon the wintry landscape, and I, at least, was oblivious to all else but the fact that I was talking with the woman whose interest for me was paramount, when a lump of coal fell from the grate upon the fire-irons.

We both turned, and saw Herod Voltaire standing by a bookcase with an open volume in his hand. A disinterested person might have fancied he had not heard a word of our conversation, but I was sure I saw a steely glitter in his eyes, and a cruel smile playing around his mouth.

"Then you go to church this morning?" I said, seeking to turn the conversation as naturally as I could.

"Yes, I always do on Christmas morning," she replied, as if thankful I had given her an opportunity of speaking about other matters.

"Then I hope I shall have the pleasure of escorting you," I replied.

Ordinarily I should not have dared to mention such a matter to a lady I had seen so little of, but the request slipped out unthinkingly; and she, no doubt confused by the presence of Voltaire, cheerfully assented.

Our embarrassment came to an end just then, for several others came into the room, and the conversation became general.

As the reader may guess, I was highly elated at the turn matters were taking, and in my heart I began to laugh at Voltaire's idea of winning Gertrude Forrest. Moreover, she had willingly consented to walk to church with me, and had expressed a dislike for the man I, in spite of myself, was beginning to fear.

Only a very few of the party found their way to the old time-honoured building to join in the Christmas service that morning. Some were tired and remained in their rooms, while others enjoyed sitting around the cheerful fires. I was not sorry, however, for I was thus enabled to enjoy more of Miss Forrest's society. Need I say that my morning was truly enjoyable? I think not. I found in my companion one who was in every way delightful. Widely read, she was able to converse about books she loved, and possessing a mind that was untrammelled by society notions, it was refreshing to hear her talk. Far removed from the giddy society girl, she was yet full of mirth and pleasantness. Ready witted, she was quick at repartee; and possessing a keen sense of humour, she saw enjoyment in that which to many would be commonplace.

Only one thing marred my happiness. That was the memory of a cruel look which rested on Voltaire's face as we went away together. From that moment I am sure he regarded me as his rival, and from that moment he sought to measure his strength with mine. I could see in his face that he had guessed my secret, while I fancied I could see, beneath his somewhat cynical demeanour, indications of his love for Gertrude Forrest.

On our way back from church we met Voltaire and Kaffar, who were eagerly conversing. They took but little notice of us, however, and, for my own part, I felt relieved when they were out of sight.

"Do you know what is on the programme for to-night?" I said, when they were out of hearing.

"Yes; Mr. Temple has arranged for a conjuror and a

ventriloquist to come, and thus we shall have something to occupy our attention besides ordinary chitchat."

"I'm very glad," I replied, "although I should be delighted to spend the evening as I have spent this morning."

I said this with an earnestness about which there could be no doubt, and I fancied I saw a blush mount to her cheek. At any rate, I felt that we were good friends, and my heart beat high with hope.

Arriving at Temple Hall, I saw Tom reading a letter. "Disappointing, Justin, my boy," he said.

"What's the matter?" I asked.

"Why, I engaged some fellows to come here and give us an entertainment to-night, and they write to say they can't come. But never mind; we must do the best we can among ourselves. You are good at all sorts of odd games; while at— yes, the very thing!—that's delightful!"

"What's delightful?"

"You'll know to-night! 'Pon my word, it's lucky those juggling fellows can't come. Anyhow, I can promise you a jolly evening."

Had I known then what that evening would lead to, I should not have entered the house so joyously as I did; but I knew nothing of what lay in the future, while Miss Forrest's great dark eyes beamed upon me in such a way as to make earth seem like heaven.

CHAPTER IV

VOLTAIRE'S STORY OF THE EAST

When lunch-time came, I, to my delight, obtained a seat next to Miss Forrest, and soon I became oblivious to all else but her. I was sure, too, that she liked me. Her every word and action disclaimed the idea of her being a coquette, while her honest preference for my society was apparent.

As we left the table I turned towards Voltaire, and I found that he was looking at us. If ever hate and cruelty were expressed in any human face, they were expressed in his. Evidently he regarded me as his rival, and thus his natural enemy. A little later in the afternoon he was again talking with Kaffar, and instinctively I felt that I was the subject of his conversation. But I did not trouble, for was not Gertrude Forrest near me, and did we not have delightful conversation together? It seemed as if we had known each other for years, and thus it was natural for us to converse freely.

Just before dinner, Voltaire came to me, as if he wished to enter into conversation. He commenced talking about Yorkshire, its customs, legends, and superstitions, and then, with a tact and shrewdness which I could not resist, he drew me into a talk about myself. I felt that he was sifting me, felt that he was trying to read my very soul, and yet I could not break myself from him.

One thing was in my favour. I knew his feelings towards me, felt sure that he hated me, and thus I kept on my guard. Time after time, by some subtle question, he sought to lead me to speak about the woman dear to my heart, but in that he did not succeed. He fascinated me, and in a degree mastered me, but did not succeed in all his desires. I knew he was weighing me, testing me, and seeking to estimate my powers, but being on my guard his success was limited.

When our conversation ceased I felt sure of one thing. It was to be a fight to the death between me and this man, if I would obtain the woman I loved. Perhaps some may think this conclusion to be built on a very insufficient foundation, nevertheless I felt sure that such was the case. When I was quite a lad, I remember an old Scotchwoman visited our house. It is little I can recall to memory now concerning her, but I know that when she first set her eye upon me she said—

"Eh, Mrs. Blake, but yon bairn has the gift o' second sight."

My mother laughed at the idea, whereupon the old woman began to correct herself.

"I'll no say he has the gift o' second sight properly," she said, "but he'll *feel* in a minute what it'll tak soom fowk years to fin' out. Eh, lad"—turning to me—"if ye coom across some one as ye doesna like, hae as leetle to do wi' 'em as ye can."

I am inclined to think there is truth in this judgment of the old Scotch lady. I have found her words true in many cases, and I was sure in the case of Voltaire my feelings told me what actually existed.

There was one thing in my favour. Evidently he did not think I guessed his wishes; nevertheless I felt sure that if I was to obtain the mastery over such a man, it would be little short of a miracle.

Dinner passed over without anything worthy of note, but as soon as it was over we hurried to the drawing-room. Even those who loved their after-dinner wine joined the ladies, as if in expectation of something wonderful. The truth was, it had gone around that Mr. Voltaire was going to tell us a story concerning the mystic rites that are practised in Eastern lands, and the subject was an attractive one. The ladies especially, evidently fascinated by the witchery of this man's presence, anxiously waited for him to commence.

"What do you wish me to tell you about?" he said in answer to repeated requests for him to begin, from several young ladies.

"Oh, tell us a story of second sight, and spiritualism, and all that, you know," replied a young lady with a doll's face and simpering manner.

"You promised you would," said another.

"True, I promised, but not to-day. This Christmas Day is like Sunday to you English folk, and I do not wish to mar its sacredness."

"Oh, the Sunday part of it is all ended at twelve o'clock," cried the young lady who had spoken first. "As soon as church is over we commence our fun. Do, Mr. Voltaire; we shall be disappointed if you don't."

"I cannot resist the ladies," he said, with a smile, "but you must not be frightened at my story. For, remember, what I tell you is true. I do not weave this out of my own brain like your average English novelist has to do."

I fancied this was directed at me. Not that I deserved the appellation. I had written only one novel, and that was a very poor one. Still I fancied I saw his light glittering eyes turned in my direction.

"I must make a sort of apology, too," he went on. "Many of you do not believe in what will be the very marrow of my story."

"Come, Voltaire, never mind apologies," said Tom Temple; "we are all anxious to hear it."

"I mentioned last night," said Voltaire, "that I had spent some time in Egypt up by the Nile. The story I have to tell relates to that part of the world.

"I had sailed up the Nile, by one of the ordinary river steamers, to a place called Aboo Simbel, close to the Second Cataract. Here the ordinary tourist stops, and stops too at the beginning of what really interests an imaginative mind. There are, however, some fine ruins here which well repay one for a visit. Ah me! *One* wishes he had lived three or four thousand years ago when he stands among those ancient piles. There was some wisdom then, some knowledge of the deep things of life! However, I did not stay here. I went with my friend Kaffar away further into the heart of Nubia.

"I cannot speak highly of the rank and file of the people there. They are mostly degraded and uncultured, lacking"—here he bowed to the ladies—"that delightful polish which characterizes those who live in the West. Still I found some relics of the wisdom of the ancients. One of the sheiks of a village that lay buried among palm trees was deeply versed in the things I longed to know, and with him I took up my abode.

"Abou al Phadre was an old man, and not one whom the ladies would love—that is, for his face, for it was yellow and wrinkled; his eyes, too, were almost buried in their cavernous sockets, and shaded by bushy white eyebrows. Those who love the higher powers, however, and can respect the divine power of knowledge, would have knelt at Abou's feet.

"This wonderful man had a daughter born to him in his old age, born, too, with the same love for truth, the same thirst for a knowledge of things unseen to the ordinary eye. So much was this so, that she was called 'Ilfra the Understanding One.' As the years went on she outstripped her father, and obtained a knowledge of that for which her father had unsuccessfully studied all his life.

"When Kaffar and I entered this village, she was nearly twenty years of age, and was fair to look upon. It was rarely she spoke to me, however, for she dwelt with the unseen and talked with the buried dead. Abou, on the other hand, was kind to me, and taught me much, and together we tried to find out what for years he had been vainly searching. What that secret was I will not tell. Only those who live in the atmosphere of mystery can think rightly about what lies in the mind and heart of the true magician.

"As I before hinted, 'Ilfra the Understanding One' had found out the secret; her soul had outsoared that of her father and of all the sages for many miles around, and she would have revealed her knowledge both to her father and to me, but for one thing. Seven is a perfect number, and all the Easterns take it into consideration, and it is a law that no one shall reveal a secret that they may have found until three times seven years pass over their heads. Thus it was, while we eagerly sought for the mysterious power I have mentioned, we were buoyed up by the hope that, though we might not be successful, Ilfra would reveal to us what we desired to know."

"And thus the time passed on until we reached Ilfra's twenty-first birthday, with the exception of seven days. Both Abou and I were glad at heart; for although the secret, to me, would be as nothing compared to what it would be to him, yet I could put it to some use, while, to him, it would dispel distance, time, and physical life. Through it the secrets of astronomer and astrologer would be known, while the pages of the past would lie before him like an open book.

"Judge his anguish then, and my disappointment, when, seven days before her twenty-first birthday, she was bitten by a cerastes, and her body died. Had she been near her home, her knowledge would have defied the powers of this most deadly serpent's bite; for she knew antidotes for every poison. As it was, however, the same kind of serpent that had laid the beautiful Cleopatra low, likewise set at liberty the soul of Ilfra. Do not think Abou grieved because of her death. Death was not death to him—his eyes pierced that dark barrier; he suffered because the glorious knowledge he longed for was rudely snatched from him."

"'Thou man of the West who bearest the name of a Jewish king,' he said to me, 'this is a heavy blow.'"

"'Not too heavy for you, Abou,' I said. 'The soul has flown, but when the three times seven years is complete you can call her back and learn her wisdom.'"

"'I can call her back, but the secret—ah, I know it not,' he said."

By this time there was a deadly silence in the room. Every ear was strained, so that not one sound of Voltaire's voice might be missed. As for him, he sat with his eyes fixed, as if he saw beyond the present time and place, while his face was like a piece of marble. Kaffar, I noticed, fixed his eyes upon his friend, and in his stony stare he seemed possessed of an evil spirit.

None of the English guests spoke when Voltaire stopped a second in his narration. All seemed afraid to utter a sound, except Kaffar.

"Go on, Herod," he said; "I am up in Egypt again."

"It was little we ate," said Voltaire, "during the next seven days. We were too anxious to know whether the secrets of the dead were to be revealed. Neither could we speak much, for the tongue is generally silent when the soul is wrapped in mystery; and right glad were we when the day dawned on which the veil should be made thicker or altogether drawn aside.

"We did not seek to know the mystery after which we were panting until the midnight of Ilfra's birthday. Then, when the earth in its revolution spelt out that hour, we entered the room of the maiden whose soul had departed.

"The Egyptians have lost much of the knowledge of the ancients, especially in the art of embalming. Often the sons of Egypt moan over that departed wisdom; still the art is not altogether gone. The body of Ilfra lay embalmed before us as we entered. She had been beautiful in life, but was more beautiful in death, and it was with reverence for that beauty that I stood beside her.

"'Fetch Helfa,' said Abou to a servant, 'and then begone.'"

"Helfa was Abou's son. Here, in England, you would cruelly designate him as something between a madman and an idiot, but the Easterns look not thus upon those who possess not their ordinary faculties. Through Helfa, Abou had seen many wonderful things, and now he was going to use him again.

"'Howajja Herod,' he said to me, 'I am first going to use one of our old means of getting knowledge. It has failed me in the past, but it will be, perchance, more potent in the presence of Ilfra the Understanding One.'"

"With that he took some ink, and poured it in Helfa's hand. This ink was the most precious in his possession, and obtained by means not lawful to relate. When it was in his son's hands he looked at me straight in the eyes, until, while I was in possession of all my senses, I seemed to live a charmed life. My imagination soared, my heart felt a wondrous joy.

"'Look,' said Abou, 'look in Helfa's hand.'"

"I looked intently."

"'What see you, son Herod?'"

"'I see a paradise,' I replied, 'but I cannot describe it. The beauties are incomparable. Ilfra is there; she mingles with those who are most obeyed.'"

"'See you anything by which the mystery can be learned?'

"'I can see nothing.'"

"I heard a sigh. I had returned to my normal condition again, and had told nothing."

"'I expected this,' he said, 'but I will try Helfa.'"

"The experiment with Helfa, however, was just as fruitless."

"Then he turned to me. 'Son Herod,' he said, 'prepare to see the greatest deed ever done by man. All the knowledge and power of my life are to be concentrated in one act.'"

"With that he looked at Helfa, who staggered to a low cushion."

"'Spirit of Helfa, leave the body,' he said."

"Instantly the eyes of Helfa began to close; his limbs grew stiff, and in a few seconds he lay lifeless by us."

"'I have a mission for you, spirit of Helfa. Flee to the home of spirits, and bring back the soul of thy sister, that she may tell me what we wish to know.'"

"When the command was given, I felt that a something—an entity—was gone from us. Abou and I were alone with the two bodies.

"'What expect you, Abou?' I said, anxiously."

"'If the labour of a lifetime has not been a failure,' he said, 'these two bodies will soon possess their spirits.'"

Again Voltaire stopped in his recital, and looked around the room. He saw that every eye was fixed upon him, while the faces of some of the young ladies were blanched with terror. Evidently they were deeply moved. Even some of the young men shuddered, not so much because of the story that was told, as the strange power of the man that told it. As he saw these marks of interest, a smile crept over his face. He evidently felt that he was the strongest influence in the room—that all had to yield to him as their superior.

"I confess," he went on, "that my heart began to beat quickly at these words. Fancy, if you can, the scene. An Egyptian village, not far removed from some of the great temples of the dead past. Above our heads waved tall palm trees. Around was a strange land, and a wild, lawless people. The hour was midnight, and our business was with the dead.

"We had not waited above three minutes when I knew that the room was peopled—by whom I knew not, except that they came from that land from whose bourne, your greatest poet says, 'no traveller returns.' I looked at Abou. His face was as the face of the dead, except for his eyes. They burned like two coals of fire. He uttered some strange words, the meaning of which was unknown to me, and then I knew some mighty forces were being exerted in that old sheik's hut. My brain began to whirl, while a terrible power gripped me; but still I looked, and still I remembered.

"'Spirit of Ilfra,' said Abou, 'are you here?'"

"No voice spoke that I could hear, and yet I realized that Abou had received his answer."

"'Enter thy body then, spirit of my daughter, and tell me, if thou darest, the secret I have desired so long.'"

"I looked at the embalmed body. I saw the eyelids quiver, the mouth twitch, and then the body moved."

"'Speak to me, my daughter, and tell me all,' said Abou."

"I only heard one sound. My overtaxed nerves could bear no more; the living dead was too terrible for me, and I fell senseless to the ground.

"When I awoke to consciousness, I found only Abou and Helfa there. The body of Ilfra had been removed, where, I know not, for I never saw it again; but Helfa was like unto that which he had been before.

"'The secret is mine, son Herod,' said Abou, 'but it is not for you to learn yet. Be patient; when your spirit is prepared, the knowledge will come.'"

Voltaire stopped abruptly. One of the young ladies gave a slight scream, and then he apologized for having no more to tell.

"But has the knowledge come since?" asked a voice.

I did not know who spoke, but it sounded like Gertrude Forrest's voice. I turned towards her, and saw her looking admiringly at this man whom I could not help fearing.

His answer was a beaming smile and a few words, saying that knowledge should never be boasted of.

That moment my jealousy, which had been allayed, now surged furiously in me, and I determined that that very night I would match the strength of my mind with the strength of his.

CHAPTER V

CHRISTMAS NIGHT—THE FORGING
OF THE CHAIN

"You have more than redeemed your promise, Voltaire," said Tom Temple, after a silence that was almost painful. "Certainly there is enough romance and mystery in your story to satisfy any one. What do you think of it, Justin?"— turning to me.

"Mr. Voltaire used the word 'imagination' in his story," I replied, "and I think it would describe it very well. Still, it does not account for much after one has read Dumas' *Memoirs of a Physician.*"

"Am I to understand that you doubt the truth of my words?" asked Voltaire sharply.

"I think your story is all it appears to be," I replied.

Honestly, however, I did not believe in one word of it. On the very face of it, it was absurd. The idea of taking a spirit from a living body and sending it after some one that was dead, in order that some secret might be learned, might pass for a huge joke; but certainly it could not be believed in by any well-balanced mind. At any rate, such was my conviction.

"I have heard that Mr. Blake has attempted to write a novel," said Voltaire. "Perhaps he believes my story is made on the same principle."

"Scarcely," I replied. "My novel was a failure. It caused no sensation at all. Your story, on the other hand, is a brilliant success. See with what breathless interest it was listened to, and how it haunts the memories of your hearers even yet!"

This raised a slight titter. I do not know why it should, save that some of the young ladies were frightened, and accepted the first opportunity whereby they could in some way relieve their feelings. Anyhow it aroused Mr. Voltaire, for, as he looked at me, there was the look of a demon in his face, and his hand trembled.

"Do you doubt the existence of the forces I have mentioned?" he asked. "Do you think that the matters to which I have referred exist only in the mind? Are they, in your idea, no sciences in reality?"

"Pardon me, Mr. Voltaire," I replied, "but I am an Englishman. We are thought by foreigners to be very conservative, and perhaps there may be truth in it. Anyhow, I, for one, like tangible proof before I believe in anything that does not appeal to my reason. Your story does not appear reasonable, and, although I hope I do not offend you by saying so, I cannot accept it as gospel."

"Perhaps," said Kaffar, who spoke for the first time, "Mr. Blake would like some proofs. Perhaps he would like not only to *see* manifestations of the power of the unseen, but to *feel* them. Ah! pardon me, ladies and gentlemen, but I cannot stand by and hear the greatest of all sciences maligned, and still be quiet. I cannot be silent when that which is dearer to me than life itself is submitted to the cool test of bigoted ignorance. You may not believe it true, but I would give much to know what Ilfra the Understanding One knew. I was reared under Egypt's sunny skies; I have lain under her stately palms and watched the twinkling stars; I am a child of the East, and believe in the truths that are taught there. I have only dabbled in the mysteries of the unseen, but I know enough to tell you that what my friend says is true."

Was this a ruse on the part of the Egyptian? Looking at the whole matter in the light of what followed I believe it was. And yet at the time I did not know.

"I am sorry," I replied, "if I have caused annoyance. But we English people possess the right of our opinions. However, I do not wish to bias other minds, and trust that my scepticism may cause no unpleasantness."

"But would Mr. Blake like to be convinced?" said Voltaire.

"I am perfectly indifferent about the matter," I replied.

"That is very convenient for one who has stated his beliefs so doggedly. Certainly I do not think that is English; if it is, I am glad I am not an Englishman."

With this he fixed his eyes steadily on me, and tried to fasten my attention, but did not at the time succeed.

"I was asked for my opinion," I said; "I did not force it. But still, since you place it in that light, I *should* like to be convinced."

By this time the interest manifested in the matter was great. Every one watched breathlessly for what was to be done or said next, and certainly I felt that I was regarded by the guests in anything but a favourable light.

I saw Voltaire and Kaffar exchanging glances, and I felt sure that I heard the former say in Arabic, "Not yet."

After this the two arranged to give us some manifestations of their power. While they were conversing I went across the room and spoke to Miss Forrest; but she was very reserved, and I thought her face looked very pale.

"This is becoming interesting," I said.

"I wish you had said nothing about his story," was her reply.

"Pray why?"

She only shook her head.

"Surely you do not believe in his foolish story or conjuring tricks?" I said laughingly.

But she did not reply in the same vein.

"Mr. Voltaire is a wonderful man," she said, "a clever man. If I were a man I should not like to make him my enemy."

"I have heard of an old saying at my home," I replied, "which ran something like this, 'Brag is a good dog, but Holdfast is better.'"

"Still I should have nothing to do with Brag," she said.

"I hope you will not," I replied meaningly.

She did not answer me, but I fancied she blushed; and again I felt happy.

By this time Voltaire was ready with his performance. "You

Joseph Hocking

will see," he said, "that here we have no chance for stage tricks. All is plain and open as the day. Moreover, I will have no secrets from you even with regard to the subject itself. The phenomena that will be brought before you are purely psychological. The mind of my friend Kaffar will be, by a secret power, merged into mine. What I see he will see, although in your idea of the matter he does not see at all. Now, first of all, I wish you to blindfold my friend Kaffar. Perhaps Mr. Blake, seeing he longs for truth, may like to do this. No? Well, then, perhaps our host will. Thank you, Mr. Temple."

With this Tom Temple completely blindfolded the Egyptian, and then we awaited the further development of the matter.

"Would you mind leading him to the library?" Voltaire continued. "He will certainly not be able to see anything of us here, and still he will not be out of earshot."

Kaffar was accordingly led into the library, blindfolded.

"Now," said Voltaire, "I told you that by a secret power his mind and mine became one. I will prove to you that I have not spoken boastingly. Will any gentleman or lady show me any curiosity he or she may have?"

Accordingly several of the party pulled from their pockets articles of interest, and of which neither Voltaire nor Kaffar could have known. Each time the former asked what the article was, and each time the latter, although at a distance, correctly described it.

A look of wonder began to settle on the faces of the guests, and exclamations of surprise and bewilderment were apparent. It was apparent that nearly all were converts to his beliefs, if beliefs they might be called. After a number of articles were shown and described, Kaffar was recalled, and was loudly applauded.

"You see," said Voltaire, "the evident truth of this. Certainly this is a very simple affair, and my old friend Abou al Phadre would have smiled at its littleness. Still it must convince every unprejudiced mind that there is something deeper and more wonderful than those things which are constantly passing before your view."

Miss Staggles, who had been almost as silent as a sphinx, spoke now. "We are convinced that you are a wonderful man," she said; "and what I have seen to-night will be ever a matter of marvel, as well as thankfulness that I have been privileged to see it."

This was evidently the opinion of every one in the room. Even Gertrude Forrest was carried away by it, while Miss Edith Gray was enraptured at what she termed "a glorious mystery."

"I should like," said Miss Staggles, "to hear what Mr. Blake, the Thomas of the party, has to say to it."

There was an ugly leer in the old woman's eye as she spoke, and the thought struck me that Voltaire had been making friends with her.

"Yes," said Voltaire; "I am sure we should all like to know whether Mr. Blake is convinced."

"I am convinced that Mr. Kaffar has a good memory," I said.

"Good memory! What do you mean?"

"Why, Mr. Voltaire and his friends have come a few years

too late to make a good impression. I have not only seen a better performance at a dozen entertainments, but I have found out the secret of what is called 'thought-reading.'"

"Do you mean to say you have seen similar feats before?" asked Voltaire, savagely.

"At least a dozen times," I replied. "In a few years' time, we shall see the like performed on the sands at our fashionable watering-places."

"I am glad," said Kaffar, "that the education of your country has so far advanced."

I went on talking, not realizing that I was all the time forging a chain that should hold me in cruel bondage. "I am afraid it says very little for our education," I replied. "Some clever fellow has invented a clever system for asking and answering questions, and those who have taken the trouble to learn it have been able to deceive a credulous public."

Voltaire's eyes flashed fire. All the malignity and cruelty that could be expressed in a human face I thought I saw expressed in his. And yet he wore his old fascinating smile; he never lost his seeming self-possession.

"I must deny Mr. Blake's statement," he said; "and, further, I would defy him to find or produce such a code of questions as he mentions."

I immediately left the room, and soon afterwards returned with a book by a renowned thought-reader, wherein he explained what, to so many, has appeared marvellous. I pointed out how, according to his system, by asking a question, the first word of which should begin with a certain letter, a particular thing should be indicated, and all that would be needed was that the performers should be perfectly conversant with the system.

The company quickly saw the truth of what I was saying, and for the time, at any rate, Mr. Voltaire's marvellous knowledge was held at a discount. "But does Mr. Blake mean to insinuate that Mr. Kaffar and myself have learnt such a code as this?" said Voltaire at length.

"I insinuate nothing," I replied. "I am simply showing how your performance can be done by those possessing no knowledge of the occult sciences."

"But does Mr. Blake decline to believe that we know nothing of the mysterious—that we have not dived into subjects of which the ordinary mind can know nothing?" said Kaffar.

"Pardon me," I replied, "but I decline to answer. I have not volunteered any opinion either as to Mr. Voltaire's story or your performance. I was asked my opinion, and I gave it."

I watched Mr. Voltaire's face as I spoke. He seemed to be pondering some matter in his mind, and appeared irresolute as to what action he should take. At length, a strange light shot from his eyes, and he raised his head and spoke.

"Ladies and gentlemen," he said, "evidently Mr. Blake, with his hard English common-sense, has raised some amount of doubt in your minds as to the validity of my story and of our performance. I am sure you will allow me to vindicate and prove any assertion I have made. If I have claimed a knowledge of the mysterious, I have not done so without reason."

"We believe that is true," said Miss Staggles; "we believe you are a wonderful man."

"Thank you," said Voltaire. "I am sure I have Miss Staggles' sympathies, but will some one assist me in what I am about to do? I will allow no possibility of a *system* in this, and consequently I shall be glad if any gentleman will help me in the manifestation of the hidden powers of the human mind. Perhaps"—turning, I thought, eagerly to me—"Mr. Blake will be the one?"

"No," I said; "I prefer to be a spectator."

I could no longer mistake the hate that flashed from his eyes; but he said nothing, and waited quietly for a volunteer. No one was forthcoming. At length Tom Temple said—

"Would one of the servants do, Voltaire?"

"I would rather have a visitor," said Voltaire, "and for two reasons: first, you could not then have any reason for suspecting a collusion; and, second, the ordinary English servant is extremely unsusceptible to the play of higher powers. If, however, none of you will volunteer, I can see no other alternative."

Accordingly, a man about my own age was brought in, and introduced as Simon Slowden. I saw that he was no ordinary character as soon as he entered, and was by no means one who could be easily imposed upon. I afterwards found that Simon had spent his boyhood in London, had when a youth joined a travelling circus, and tramped the country for a few years. He had also travelled with several "shows," two or three travelling theatres, and had finally settled down with a lame leg at Temple Hall, where he made himself generally useful.

His dialect was a mixture of the Cockney and a dozen others equally bad, until it was almost impossible to tell from that source the part of the country from which he hailed. He was, however, a good-hearted fellow, and for a wonder, considering his history, as honest as the day.

"Now, Simon," said Tom Temple, "this gentleman is a scientist and wants to show some experiments, and he can't get any one to assist him, so I thought I'd ask you."

"Well," said Simon, "I don't know as I think mich on these science gents. They're allays a-bringin' in some new-fangled thing or other, but generally there's nowt in 'em. Still, to 'blige the company, I'll do owt raisonable. I'm tough has a crocodile's tongue, and can stand a goodish bit o' jingo and nonsense. Here goes, yer honour." Voltaire eyed him doubtfully, and Simon coolly returned the stare.

"You are not a-gwine to waccinate me, be 'ee?" said Simon at length.

"No—why?"

"'Cause I can't stand that, tough as I be. I lived wi' a doctor once, and says he to me, 'Simon, I want to speriment on ye,' says he. 'I'm tough 'nough,' says I. 'I want to waccinate you 'gainst cholera, hoopin' cough, and small-pox,' says he. 'What's that? give 'em to me?' says I. 'No,' says he, 'but to prevent you from a hevin' 'em.' 'That's yer sorts,' says I. Well, gentlemen, he waccinated me, and I said to un, 'Never no more, yer honour.'"

"Why?" asked I.

"'Cause I'd rather hev cholera, hoopin' cough, and small-pox all together than be waccinated. Jes like women, you never know where they'll break out."

"Will you kindly sit down," said Voltaire, "while I go to my room for a book?"

While he was gone I went to Simon, and spoke to him, and that gentleman got very communicative.

"I'm not overmich in love wi' that chap," he says; "and sure's I'm a right-down Cockney, he hates you like pizen. Give 'im a wide berth, yer honour, and doan't hev nothin' to do wi' 'im."

"Oh," I replied, "he can't hurt me."

"Don't know, yer honour. You and he's got your peepers fixed in the same place, and scuse me; but if you give 'im a chance, he'll beat yer. He'd charm a serpiant vith thews peepers o' hisn."

"Aren't you afraid yourself, then?"

"He can't hurt me, for I'm too tough, and I'm noan sighin' for anybody, I ain't; and I hain't a got a good-lookin' jib, and—"

But here Voltaire entered the room and spoke to Tom Temple.

"Simon," said Tom a second after, "what colour are the chestnut mare's eyes?"

Simon heaved himself, struggled, looked vacant, and said dreamily, "They're loike women, and—waccination, you—you—" But a film came over his eyes, and he was unconscious.

Again there was deathly silence in the room, and all eyes were turned towards Voltaire, who had walked close to

Simon Slowden.

"The man is not very susceptible," said Voltaire, "consequently I cannot do so much with him as I should had he been more highly organized; but I can at least convince sceptics. You will see," he went on, "that I have not touched him, and yet he is no longer conscious. I will now ask him any question, concerning either the dead or the living, that you may be inclined to ask."

"I will ask a test question," said Gertrude Forrest. "What are the servants doing at this time?"

"The cook's examinin' a goose," was the reply, "and the housemaid's talking wi' a chap as is just come from t' village."

He went on telling what the rest were doing; but Tom Temple immediately sent to the kitchen, and found that things were as was described.

"Where's Dr. Sharp?" said Mrs. Temple, adding that they could easily find out the doctor's present whereabouts the next day.

"He's comin' up here with his long-nosed pointer," was the reply, "and 'll be 'ere in a jiffy."

Five minutes after, Dr. Sharp came into the room. "I did not know I could come until half-an-hour ago," he said as he entered, and then stared as he saw how matters stood.

"Will you tell me," said Miss Forrest, "what my aunt is doing just now?"

She mentioned no name, and I do not know how the man

Joseph Hocking

sitting in the chair could know anything about her.

"She is jest gwine to bed," he said; "she's a bit ov a cold in 'er chest, and housekeeper is gwine to take some warmin' stuff to her."

"I'll know if this is true to-morrow," said Miss Forrest, and then relapsed into silence.

Meanwhile question after question was asked and answered, while Voltaire and Kaffar stood side by side, each with a terrible glitter in his eyes.

Under some secret influence Simon Slowden was led to the piano, and there executed some of the latest and most difficult pieces of music, and, without hesitation, told things that were at least marvellous. Then, when excitement was at the highest, he woke up, and coolly rubbed his eyes.

No one uttered a word, we were all too much amazed. At last Voltaire, with a sidelong glance at me, asked whether we were convinced, and one by one the members of the party expressed their wonder and astonishment. I, however, was silent. Some power of obstinacy seemed to possess me. I would not tamely admit his victory, after I had openly defeated him before. Still I did not speak a word.

"Is Mr. Blake convinced?" said Miss Staggles, leering towards me.

"Of what?" I asked.

"Of Mr. Voltaire's power."

"Undoubtedly."

"Come," said Kaffar, "Mr. Blake is still a sceptic. I think it fair that he should consent to test this for himself."

"Certainly not," I replied.

"But I think it our right," said Voltaire. "You have expressed your want of faith in our power; now, if you have the courage of a man with an opinion, test the matter. Sit here as Simon did, and see whether you are right."

I thought I heard a voice saying "Don't!" close to my ear, and I hesitated.

At this there was a titter among the young ladies.

"Evidently our Thomas is afraid," said Miss Staggles.

There was an ugly look in her eyes as she said this, but the titter increased into a kind of derisive laugh.

I know it was an evidence of my cowardice, but I could not withstand their laughter. I forgot the warning voice behind me; I refused to take notice of Mrs. Temple's warning glance; I rose up, went to the chair in the middle of the room, and defiantly said, "There! do all you can with me."

Voltaire and Kaffar came up to me, while the rest crowded around. The former fixed his terrible eye upon me as if he would peer into my very soul. A strange feeling began to creep over me; but I struggled against it with all my strength, and for a minute I seemed to gain the mastery. I laughed in his face, as if I scorned his boasted strength. A strange gleam was emitted from his light grey eyes, while his lips became ashy pale. Then I saw him grip Kaffar's hand. Instantly the room was peopled with a strange crowd. Dark forms seemed to come from Voltaire's eyes; peculiar influences were all around me. The faces of the two men became dimmer and dimmer, the people appeared to float in mid air, and I with them; then something heavy seemed to move away, I thought I heard strange creeping noises, like that of an adder crawling amidst thick dry grass, and then all was blank.

CHAPTER VI

AFTERWARDS

When I awoke to consciousness I was in my bedroom. For some time I could not gather up my scattered senses; my mind refused to exercise its proper functions. Presently I heard some one speak.

"I had no idea he was so far gone," a voice said. "You see, his power of resistance is very great, and it needed four times the magnetism to bring him under that it did your servant."

"I'm sorry you experimented on him at all," said another voice.

"Oh, I can assure you no harm's done. There, you see, he's coming to."

I felt something cold at my temples, then a strange shivering sensation passed over me, and I was awake.

Voltaire, Kaffar, Tom Temple, and Simon Slowden were in the room. "How do you feel, Mr. Blake?" asked Voltaire, blandly.

I lifted my eyes to his, and felt held by a strange power. "I'm all right," I said almost mechanically, at the same time feeling as if I was under the influence of a charm.

"Then," said Voltaire, "I will leave you. Good-night."

Immediately he left, followed by Kaffar, I experiencing a sense of relief. "Did I do anything very foolish?" I asked, recollecting the events of the evening.

"Oh no, Justin," replied Tom. "And yet that Voltaire is a terrible fellow. Half the young ladies in the room were nearly as much mesmerized as you were. You acted in pretty nearly the same way as Simon here, but nothing else. Do you feel quite right?"

"I am awfully weak," I said, "and cold shivers creep down my legs."

"You were such a long time under the influence, whatever it is," said Tom. "But you'll go back to the drawing-room?"

"No; I don't feel up to it. But don't you remain. I'm feeling shaky, but I shan't mind a bit if you'll let Simon remain with me."

And so Tom left me with Simon. "Do you feel shaky and shivery, Simon?" I asked.

"Not a bit on it, sir," was the reply. "Never felt better. But 'tween you and me and the gatepost, yon hinfidel hain't a served me like he hev you. I don't like the look o' things, yer honour."

"Why, Simon?"

"Why, sir, 'tain't me as ought to tell, and yet I don't feel comfortable. I wish I could 'a had a confabulation with yer afore this performance come off. I hain't got no doubts in my mind but that hinfidel and his dootiful brother hev got dealin's with the devil."

Simon rose and went to the door, opened it, and peered cautiously around. "That Egyptian is a watcher," he said grimly, "and I don't like either of 'em."

"What's the matter, Simon?"

"Why, this yer morning, I wur exchangin' a few pleasant remarks with one of the maid-servants, when I hears the Egyptian say, 'It's gwine beautiful.' 'How?' says t'other. 'He'll nibble like hanything,' was the answer, and then I hearn a nasty sort o' laugh. Soon after, I see you with a bootiful young lady, and I see that hinfidel a-watchin' yer, with a snaky look in his eyes. And so I kep on watchin', and scuse me, yer honour, but I can guess as 'ow things be, and I'm fear'd as 'ow this waccination dodge is a trick o' this 'ere willain."

"Explain yourself, Simon."

"Well, sir, I knows as 'ow you've only bin yer one day, but I could see in a minit as 'ow you was a smitten with a certain young lady, and I can see, too, as 'ow that white-eyed willain is smitten in the same quarter, and he sees 'ow things be, and he means business."

It was by no means pleasant to hear my affairs talked of in this way, and it was a marvel to me how Simon could have learnt so much, but I have found that a certain class of English servant seems to find out everything about the house with which they are connected, and I am afraid I was very careless as to who saw the state of my feelings. At any rate,

Simon guessed how things were, and, more than that, he believed that Voltaire had some sinister design against me.

"What do you mean by what you call the vaccination dodge?" I asked, after a second's silence.

"Scuse me, yer honour, but since that doctor waccinated me and nearly killed me by it, tough as I be, I come to call all tomfoolery by the same name. I've been in theatres, yer honour, and played in pieces, and I've known the willain in the play get up a shindy like this. I knows they're on'y got up to 'arrow up the feelin's o' tender females; but I'm afeared as 'ow this Voltaire 'ev got somethin' in his head, a-concoctin' like."

"Nonsense, Simon," I said. "You are thinking about some terrible piece you've acted in, and your imagination is carrying away your judgment."

"I hope as 'ow 'tis, sur; but I don't think so. If you chop me up, sur, you'll not find sixpenno'th of imagination in my carcase, but I calcalate I'm purty 'eavy wi' judgment. Never mind, sur; Simon Slowden is in the 'ouse, if you should want help, sur."

I did not feel much inclined to talk after this, and so, dismissing Simon, I began to think of how matters stood. Certainly everything was strange. Everything, too, had been done in a hurry. It seemed to me I had lived a long life in twenty-four hours. I had fallen in love, I had made an enemy, and I had matched myself against men who possessed a knowledge of some of the secret forces of life, without ever calculating my own strength. And yet I seemed to be beating the air. Were not my thoughts concerning Voltaire's schemes about Miss Forrest all fancy? Was not I the victim of some Quixotic ideas? Was not the creation of Cervantes' brain about as sensible as I? Surely I, a man of thirty, ought to know better? And yet some things were terribly real. My love for Gertrude Forrest was real; my walk and talk with her that day were real. Ay, and the hateful glitter of Voltaire's eyes was real too; his talk with Kaffar behind the shrubs the night before was real. The biological or hypnotic power that I had felt that very night was real, and, above all, a feeling of dread that had gripped my being was real. I could not explain it, and I could not throw it off, but ever since I had awoke out of my mesmeric sleep, or whatever the reader may be pleased to call it, I felt numbed; weights seemed to hang on my limbs, and my whole being was in a kind of torpor.

I went to bed at length, however, and, after an hour's tossing, fell asleep, from which I did not wake until ten o'clock next morning. I found, on descending, that nearly all had breakfasted, but the few with whom I spoke were very kind and pleasant towards me. I had no sooner finished breakfast than I met Miss Forrest, and entered into conversation with her. Once with her, all my dreads and fears vanished. Her light eyes and merry laugh drove away dull care, and soon I was in Paradise. Surely I could not be mistaken! Surely the quivering hand, the tremulous mouth, the downcast eye, meant something! Surely she need not be agitated at meeting me, unless she took a special interest in me—unless, indeed, she felt as I felt! At any rate, it were heaven to think so. We had been talking I should think ten minutes, when Tom Temple came towards us.

"Say, Justin, my boy," he said, "what do you say to a gallop of four?"

"Who are the four?" I asked.

"Miss Forrest, Miss Edith Gray, Justin Blake, and—myself," was the reply.

"I shall be more than delighted if Miss Forrest will—" I did not finish the sentence. At that moment I felt gripped by an unseen power, and I was irresistibly drawn towards the door. I muttered something about forgetting, and then, like a man in a sleep, I put on my hat and coat and went out, I know not where.

I cannot remember much about the walk. It was very cold, and my feet crunched the frozen snow; but I thought little of it—I was drawn on and on by some secret power. I was painfully aware that Miss Forrest must think I was acting strangely and discourteously, and once or twice I essayed to go back to her, but I could not I was drawn on and on, always away from the house.

At length I entered a fir wood, and I began to feel more my real self. I saw the dark pines, from whose prickly foliage the snow crystals were falling; I realized a stern beauty in the scene; but I had not time to think about it. I felt I was near the end of my journey, and I began to wonder at my condition. I had not gone far into the wood before I stopped and looked around me. The influence had gone, and I was free; but from behind one of the trees stepped out a man, and the man was—Herod Voltaire!

"Good-morning, Mr. Justin Blake," he said blandly.

"Why have you brought me here?" I asked savagely.

He smiled blandly. "You will admit I have brought you here, then?" he said. "Ah, my friend, it is dangerous to fight with a man when you don't know his weapons."

"I want to know what this means?" I said haughtily.

"Not so fast," he sneered. "Come down from that high horse

and let's talk quietly. Yes, I've no doubt you would have enjoyed a ride with a certain lady better than the lonely walk you have had; but, then, you know the old adage, 'Needs must when the devil drives.'"

"And so you've admitted your identity!" I said. "Well, I don't want your society; say what you want to say, or I'm going back."

"Yes," he said, revealing his white teeth, "I am going to say what I want to say, and you are not going back until you have heard it, and, more than that, promised to accede to it."

Again I felt a cold shiver creep over me, but I put on a bold face, and said, "It always takes two to play at any game."

"Yes it does, Mr. Blake, and that you'll find out. You feel like defying me, don't you? Just so; but your defiance is useless. Did you not come here against your will? Are you not staying here now against your will? Look here, my man, you showed your hand immediately you came, and you've been playing your game without knowing the trump cards. It looked very innocent to be mesmerized last night, didn't it? Oh, mesmerism is a vulgar affair; but there was more than mesmerism realized last night. I played three trump cards last night, Mr. Justin Blake. The Egyptian story was one, the thought-reading was the second, the animal and mental magnetism was the third. I had tested my opponent before, and knew just how to play. When I took the last trick, you became mine—mine, body and soul!"

I still defied him, and laughed scornfully into his face.

"Yes, you laugh," he said; "but I like your English adages, and one is this, 'Those laugh best who win.' But come," he said, altering his tone, "you are in my power. By that one act last night you placed yourself in my power, and now you are my slave. But I am not a hard master. Do as I wish you, and I shall not trouble you."

"I defy you!" I cried. "I deny your power!"

"Do you?" he said. "Then try and move from your present position."

I had been leaning against a tree, and tried to move; but I could not. I was like one fastened to the ground.

He laughed scornfully. "Now do you believe?" he said.

I was silent.

"Yes," he said, "you may well be silent, for what I say is true. And now," he continued, "I promise not to use my power over you on one condition."

"Name it," I said.

"I will name it. It is this. You must give up all thoughts, all hopes, all designs, of ever winning Gertrude Forrest for your wife."

"And if I refuse?"

"If you refuse, I shall have to make you do what I would rather you would do willingly. Think as you will, but she can never be yours. I do not mind telling you now, for you dare not speak. I have marked her for my own; and, mark you, she must be mine. No power shall stop that. If you presume to speak to her, I will stop you in the act. If ever you seek to walk with her, I will drag you away from her; nay, more than that, I will make you act in such a way as to make you, to her, an object of derision."

"But," I said, "if you possess such a power over me, which I do not admit, I will proclaim to every one in the house the villainous means by which you have possessed it. I will make you an object of hatred."

His light eyes gleamed with an unearthly glare. "Think you I have not thought of that?" he said. "Try and tell of my influence over you, seek to speak one word against me, and mark the result. I defy you to utter one word."

Again I was silent. I seemed hemmed in on every hand by this man's terrible power. "Come," he said, "do you consent to my terms? Do you relinquish all thoughts, all hopes, of ever winning Gertrude Forrest?"

In spite of my strange situation, I could not help seeing two rays of light. One was, that this man must have seen that Miss Forrest looked on me with a degree of favour; and the other was that, if his power was as great as he boasted, he needed not be so anxious to obtain my consent to his terms. If I were wholly in his power, he could do with me as he would, and need not trouble about any promises of mine. This led me to defy him still.

"Herod Voltaire," I said, "villain by your own admission, I do not believe in your power; but, admitting it for the moment, I still refuse to do what you ask me. You have guessed my secret. I love Gertrude Forrest with all my heart, and I will promise neither you nor any other man to give up hopes of winning her. And mark you this, too. Although by unlawful means you may have obtained mastery over me, as surely as there is a God who cares for men, your power will be broken. Meanwhile, you may force me to act against my will, but my will you shall never have!"

"Fool, idiot!" he cried, "you shall repent this. You shall be dragged through mire, dirt, pain, defeat, disgrace, and then, when all is over, you will find I have had my own way!" He made a step towards me. "Stay there for a quarter of an hour," he said, "and then you may go where you will."

He rushed away, and left me alone. I tried to move, but could not; and yet I realized this—although my body was chained, my mind was still free and active. When the quarter of an hour was up, I went away, with a great weight upon my heart, wondering, yet dreading, what would happen next.

CHAPTER VII

DREARWATER POND

I will not try to describe my walk back to Temple Hall, or tell of the terrible sensations that I felt. Think, if you can, of my position. A young man of thirty, a slave to a deep designing villain, held fast in his power by some secret nervous or brain forces which he possessed. More than this, he had designs upon the woman I loved, while I was powerless, nay, worse than powerless, for he might make me do things which would be altogether opposed to what I believed right and true. When you realize this, you will be able to form some idea of how I felt. And yet I 'was not altogether without hope. I felt that life and love of liberty were strong in me, and I determined that, though I might be conquered, it should not be without a struggle.

Arriving at the house, I saw Simon Slowden. He evidently had a message for me, for, making a sign for me to stop, he quickly came to my side.

"Yer nag is saddled, sur," he said.

I caught his meaning instantly. "Which way did they go, and how long have they been gone?" I asked.

Joseph Hocking

"They're gone to Drearwater Pond, yer honour. Started 'bout half-an-hour ago."

"Any message for me?"

"The guv'nor told me, if I saw yer, to tell yer where they'd gone."

"Who went with Mr. Temple?"

"Miss Gray and the other lady, yer honour."

He had led out the horse by this time, and I was preparing to mount it, when I saw that he had something more to communicate.

"What is it, Simon?" I said.

He did not speak, but winked slyly at me, and then led the horse away from the stable-yard. As he did so, I saw Kaffar come away from one of the lads who was employed about the house.

"He's a spy, yer honour, a reg'lar Judas Iscariot. T'other chap's called Herod, pity this one isn't called Judas. They be a bootiful couple, yer honour." He looked around again, and then said, "That murderin', waccinatin' willain is gone efter 'em, Mr. Blake. He came back just after they'd gone, and went ridin' efter 'em like greased lightnin'."

For a minute I was stunned.

"I thought I'd better tell 'ee, yer honour, and then you'd know 'ow to act."

I thanked Simon heartily; then, turning my horse's head

towards Drearwater Pond, I galloped away. I had not gone far before I began to question the wisdom of what I was doing. Was I right in thus openly defying the man who possessed such a terrible power? It certainly seemed foolish, and yet I could not bear the idea of his being the companion of Gertrude Forrest. Besides, it might stagger him somewhat to find that his words had not frightened me.

With this thought I gave my horse the rein. He was a beautiful high-blooded creature, and seemed to delight in making the snow crystals fly around him, as he scampered over the frozen ground.

I did not know the district at all, but I had been told in what direction Drearwater Pond lay, so I did not doubt that I should easily find them. When I came to the spot, however, those I hoped to find were nowhere to be seen, and so, guiding the horse up to the dark waters, I stood and looked at the little lake that bore such a sombre name. It was indeed a dreary place. On one side was wild moorland, and on the other a plantation of firs edged the dismal pond. It might be about a quarter of a mile long, and perhaps one-sixth of a mile wide. There were no houses near, and the high-road was some distance away. It was not an attractive place for several reasons. The region was very drear, and, moreover, the place had a bad reputation. The pond was said to have no bottom, while a murder having been committed on the moors near by, the country people said that dark spirits of the dead were often seen to float over the Drearwaters in the silent night.

I stood at the edge of the water for some time; then I quietly led my horse away around to the other side, where dark fir trees made the scene, if possible, more gloomy than it would otherwise have been. I had not been there long before I heard voices, and, looking up, I saw the party walking towards me. Evidently they had fastened their horses in the near distance, and were now seeking to better enjoy themselves by walking.

As they came near me, I made a slight noise, which drew their attention. Certainly I ought to have felt flattered by their greeting, especially, by that of Miss Forrest.

"We thought you had been bewitched, Mr. Blake," said Miss Gray, after a few trivial remarks had been passed.

"Perhaps I was," I said, looking at Voltaire. He stared at me as if in wonder, and a curious light played in his eyes. He had uttered no word when he saw me, but he gave indications of his astonishment.

"Well," continued Miss Gray, "this is the proper place to be bewitched. Mr. Temple has been telling some strange stories about it. What was it, Mr. Temple?—a red hand appears from the water, and whoever sees it will be led to commit murder?"

"Oh, there are dozens of stories about the place," said Tom. "Indeed, there is scarcely a youth or maiden who will be seen here after dark."

"Why?" asked Voltaire, suddenly.

"Oh, as I said just now, it is reported to be haunted; but, more than that, the pond is said to have an evil power. Some say that if any one sees the place for the first time alone, his hands will be red with blood before a month passes away."

"Then that will refer to me," I said. "But surely such nonsense is not believed in now?"

"These things are not nonsense," said Voltaire. "Earth and

heaven are full of occult forces." I paid no further attention to the subject at the time, but this conversation came back to me with terrible force in the after-days.

For a while we chatted on ordinary subjects, and then, remounting our horses, we prepared to ride back. During this time I had felt entirely free from any of the strange influences I have described, and I began to wonder at it; especially so as Miss Forrest had voluntarily come to my side, and we had galloped away together.

We took a roundabout road to Temple Hall, and so were longer together, and again I was happy.

"I thought you were not coming," she said. "What in the world drew you away so suddenly?"

I tried to tell her, but I could not. Every time I began to speak of the influence Voltaire had exerted I was seemingly tongue-tied. No words would come.

"I was very sorry," I said at length, "but you did not want a companion. Mr. Voltaire came."

"Yes, he overtook us. Is he not a wonderful man?"

"Yes," I said absently.

"I was so sorry you allowed yourself to be placed under his influence last night. Did you not hear me asking you to avoid having anything to do with him?"

"Yes," I said, "I am sorry. I was a coward."

"I do not understand him," she said. "He fascinates while he repels. One almost hates him, and yet one is obliged to admire him. No one could want him as a friend, while to make him an enemy would be terrible."

I could not help shuddering as she spoke. I had made him my enemy, and the thought was terrible.

"He does not like you," she went on; "he did not like the way you regarded his magical story and his thought-reading. Were I you, I should have no further communications with him. I should politely ignore him."

I watched her face as she spoke. Surely there was more than common interest betrayed in her voice; surely that face showed an earnestness beyond the common interest of a passing acquaintance?

"I do not wish to have anything to do with him," I said, "and might I also say something to you? Surely if a man should avoid him, a woman should do so a thousand times more. Promise me to have nothing to do with him. Avoid him as you would a pestilence."

I spoke passionately, pleadingly. She turned her head to reply, and I was bending my head so as not to miss a word when a subtle power seized me. I did not wait for her reply, but turned my head in a different direction.

"Let us join the others," I stammered with difficulty, and rode away without waiting for her consent.

She came up by my side again presently, however, but there was a strange look on her face. Disappointment, astonishment, annoyance, and hauteur, all were expressed. I spoke not a word, however. I could not; a weight seemed to rest upon me, my free agency was gone.

"How do you know they are in this direction?" she said at length. "We have come a circuitous route."

"They surely are," I said. The words were dragged out of me, as if by sheer force of another will, while I looked vacantly before me.

"Are you well, Mr. Blake?" she asked again. "You look strange."

"Well, well," I remember saying. Then we caught sight of three people riding.

"Hurrah!" I cried, "there they are."

I could see I was surprising Miss Forrest more and more, but she did not speak again. Pride and vexation seemed to overcome her other feelings, and so silently we rode on together until we rejoined our companions.

"Ha, Justin!" cried Tom, "we did not expect to see you just yet Surely something's the matter?"

"Oh no," I replied, when, looking at Herod Voltaire, I saw a ghastly smile wreathe his lips, and then I felt my burden gone. Evidently by some strange power, at which I had laughed, he had again made me obey his will, and when he had got me where he wanted me, he allowed me to be free. No sooner did I feel my freedom than I was nearly mad with rage. I had been with the woman I wanted, more than anything else, to accompany, we had been engaged in a conversation which was getting more and more interesting for me, and then, for no reason save this man's accursed power, I had come back where I had no desire to be.

I set my teeth together and vowed to be free, but, looking

Joseph Hocking

again at Voltaire's eyes, my feelings underwent another revulsion. I trembled like an aspen leaf. I began to dread some terrible calamity. Before me stretched a dark future. I seemed to see rivers of blood, and over them floated awful creatures. For a time I thought I was disembodied, and in my new existence I did deeds too terrible to relate. Then I realized a new experience. I feared Voltaire with a terrible fear. Strange forms appeared to be emitted from his eyes, while to me his form expanded and became terrible in its mien.

I knew I was there in a Yorkshire road, riding on a high-blooded horse; I knew the woman I loved was near me; and yet I was living a dual life. It was not Justin Blake who was there, but something else which was called Justin Blake, and the feelings that possessed me were such as I had never dreamed of. And yet I was able to think; I was able to connect cause and effect. Indeed, my brain was very active, and I began to reason out why I should be so influenced, and why I should act so strangely.

The truth was, and I felt sure of it as I rode along, I was partly mesmerized or hypnotized, whatever men may please to call it. Partly I was master over my actions, and partly I was under an influence which I could not resist. Strange it may appear, but it is still true, and so while one part of my being or self was realizing to a certain extent the circumstances by which I was surrounded, the other enslaved part trembled and feared at some dreadful future, and felt bound to do what it would fain resist.

This feeling possessed me till we arrived at Temple Hall, when I felt free, and, as if by the wave of some magical wand, Justin Blake was himself again.

Instead of following the ladies into the house, I followed the horses to the stables. I thought I might see Simon Slowden, who I was sure would be my friend, and was watching Kaffar closely, but I could not catch sight of him. Herod Voltaire came up to me, however, and hissed in my ear—

"Do you yield to my power now?"

I answered almost mechanically, "No."

"But you will," he went on. "You dared to follow me to yonder lake, but you found you could not ride alone with her. How terrible it must be to have to obey the summons of the devil, and so find out the truth that while two is company, five is none!"

I began to tremble again.

He fixed his terrible eye upon me, and said slowly and distinctly, "Justin Blake, resistance is useless. I have spent years of my life in finding out the secrets of life. By pure psychology I have obtained my power over you. You are a weaker man than I—weaker under ordinary circumstances. You would be swayed by my will if I knew no more the mysteries of the mind than you, because as a man I am superior to you—superior in mind and in will-force; but by the knowledge I have mentioned I have made you my slave."

I felt the truth of his words. He was a stronger man than I naturally, while by his terrible power I was rendered entirely helpless. Still, at that very moment, the inherent obstinacy of my nature showed itself.

"I am not your slave," I said.

"You are," he said. "Did you feel no strange influences coming back just now? Was not Herod Voltaire your master?"

Joseph Hocking

I was silent.

"Just so," he answered with a smile; "and yet I wish to do you no harm. But upon this I do insist. You must leave Temple Hall; you must allow me to woo and to win Miss Gertrude Forrest."

"I never will," I cried.

"Then," said he, jeeringly, "your life must be ruined. You must be swept out of the way, and then, as I told you, I will take this dainty duck from you, I will press her rosy lips to mine, and—"

"Stop!" I cried; "not another word;" and, seizing him by the collar, I shook him furiously. "Speak lightly of her," I continued, "and I will thrash you like a dog, as well as that cur who follows at your heels."

For a moment my will had seemed to gain the mastery over him. He stared at me blankly, but only for a moment, for soon his light eyes glittered; and then, as Kaffar came up by his side, my strength was gone, my hands dropped by my side, and unheeding the cynical leer of the Egyptian, or the terrible look of his friend, I walked into the house like one in a dream.

CHAPTER VIII

DARKNESS AND LIGHT

During the next few days there was but little to record. The party evidently forgot mesmerism and thought-reading, and seemingly enjoyed themselves without its assistance. The young men and women walked together and talked together, while the matrons looked complacently on. During the day there was hunting, skating, and riding, while at night there was story-telling, charades, games of various sorts, and dancing. Altogether, it was a right old-fashioned, unconventional English country party, and day by day we got to enjoy ourselves more, because we learned to know each other better.

Perhaps, however, I am using a wrong expression. I ought not to have said "we." I cannot say that I enjoyed myself very much. My life was strange and disappointing. More than that, the calamities I dreaded did not take place, but the absence of those calamities brought me no satisfaction. And thus, while all the rest laughed and were joyful, I was solitary and sad. Once or twice I thought of leaving Temple Hall, but I could not bring myself to do so. I should be leaving the woman I was each day loving more and more, to the man who knew no honour, no mercy, no manliness.

Joseph Hocking

During these days I was entirely free from Voltaire's influence, as free as I was before I saw him. He always spoke to me politely, and to a casual observer his demeanour towards me was very friendly. Kaffar, on the other hand, treated me very rudely. He often sought to turn a laugh against me; he even greeted me with a sneer. I took no notice of him, however—never replied to his insulting words; and this evidently maddened him. The truth was, I was afraid lest there should be some design in Voltaire's apparent friendliness and Kaffar's evident desire to arouse enmity, and so I determined to be on my guard.

I was not so much surprised at my freedom from the influence he had exercised over me the day after I had placed myself under his power, and for a reason that was more than painful to me. Miss Forrest avoided ever meeting me alone, never spoke to me save in monosyllables, and was cold and haughty to me at all times. Many times had I seen her engaged in some playful conversation with some members of the party; but the moment I appeared on the scene her smile was gone, and, if opportunity occurred, she generally sought occasion to leave. Much as I loved her, I was too proud to ask a reason for this, and so, although we were so friendly on Christmas Day, we were exceedingly cold and distant when New Year's Eve came. This, as may be imagined, grieved me much; and when I saw Voltaire's smile as he watched Miss Forrest repel any attempt of mine to converse with her, I began to wish I had never set my foot in Temple Hall.

And yet I thought I might be useful to her yet. So I determined to remain in Yorkshire until she returned to London, and even then I hoped to be able to shield her from the designs which I was sure Voltaire still had.

New Year's Day was cold and forbidding. The snow had gone and the ice had melted; but the raw, biting wind swept across moor and fen, forbidding the less robust part of the company to come away from the warm fires.

I had come down as usual, and, entering the library, I found Miss Forrest seated.

"I wish you a happy new year, Miss Forrest," I said. "May it be the happiest year you have ever known." She looked around the room as if she expected to see some one else present; then, looking up at me, she said, with the happy look I loved to see, "And I heartily return your wish, Mr. Blake."

There was no coldness, no restraint in her voice. She spoke as if she was glad to see me, and wanted me to know it. Instantly a burden rolled away from my heart, and for a few minutes I was the happiest of men. Presently I heard voices at the library door, and immediately Miss Forrest's kindness and cheerfulness vanished, and those who entered the room must have fancied that I was annoying her with my company. I remained in the room a few minutes longer, but she was studiously cold and polite to me, so that when I made a pretence of going out to the stables to see a new horse Tom Temple had bought, I did so with a heavy heart.

I had no sooner entered the stable-yard than Simon Slowden appeared, and beckoned to me.

"I looked hout for yer honour all day yesterday," he said, "but you lay like a hare in a furze bush. Things is looking curious, yer honour."

"Indeed, Simon. How?"

"Can 'ee come this yer way a minit, yer honour?" "Certainly," I said, and followed him into a room over the stables. I did not like having confidences in this way; but my brain was confused, and I could not rid myself from the idea that some plot was being concocted against me.

Simon looked around to make sure there were no eaves-droppers; then he said, "There's a hancient wirgin 'ere called Miss Staggles, ain't there, Mr. Blake?"

"There is. Why?"

"It's my belief as 'ow she's bin a waccinated ten times, yer honour."

"Why, Simon?"

"Why, she's without blood or marrow, she is; and as for flesh, she ain't got none."

"Well, what for that?"

"And not honly that," he continued, without heeding my question, "she hain't a got a hounce of tender feelin's in her natur. In my opinion, sur, she's a witch, she is, and hev got dealin's with the devil."

"And what for all this?" I said. "Surely you haven't taken me up here to give me your impressions concerning Miss Staggles?"

"Well, I hev partly, yer honour. The truth is"—here he sunk his voice to a whisper—"she's very thick with that willain with a hinfidel's name. They're in league, sur." "How do you know?"

"They've bin a-promenadin' together nearly every day since Christmas; and when a feller like that 'ere Woltaire goes a-walkin' with a creature like that hancient wirgin on his arm, then I think there must be somethin' on board."

"But this is purely surmise, Simon. There is no reason why Miss Staggles and Mr. Voltaire may not walk together."

"There's more than surmise, sur. You know the plantation up behind the house, Mr. Blake?"

"The fir plantation? Very well."

"Well, sur, the night afore last I wur up there. They are hevin' a kind of Christmas-tree in one of the Sunday schools over in the willage to-night, and some o' the teachers came to the guv'nor and asked him for a tree to put some knick-knacks on. So he says to me, 'Simon,' says he, 'go up in the plantation and pull up a young fir tree, and then in the morning put it in the cart and take it over to the school-room.' This was day afore yesterday, in the afternoon. I was busy jist then, so I didn't go to the plantation till 'twas dusk. However, as you know, yer honour, 'tis moonlight, so I didn't trouble. Well, I got a young fir tree pulled up, and was jist a-going to light my pipe, when I see some figures a-comin' threw the plantation towards a summer-'ouse that was put up 'bout two year ago. So I lied luff. 'I believe,' I says, 'that it's that hinfidel and the skinny wirgin a-walkin' together.' They goes into the summer-'ouse, and then I creeps down, and gets behind a tree, but close enough to the couple to hear every word. Sure 'nough, sur, I wur right; it was the wirgin Staggles and this 'ere Woltaire.

"'They seemed quarrellin' like when I come up, for she wur sayin'—

"''Tis no use, she never will.'"

"'Nonsense!' says he. 'Give her time, and poison her mind

against that Blake, and she'll come around.'"

"'I've done that,' says she. 'I've told her that Mr. Blake is a regular male flirt; that he's had dozens of love affairs with girls; and, besides that, I told her that her marked preference for him was being talked about.'"

"'Yes,' says Woltaire, 'and see how she's treated him since.'"

"'True enough,' says she; 'but it's made her no softer towards you. If she avoids him, she dislikes you.'"

"'And do you think she cares about Blake?' says he."

"'I don't know,' she replies. 'She never would tell me anything, and that's why I dislike her so. But, for all that, she's no hypocrite.'"

"'Well, what for that?' he asks."

"'I went to her room last night, and I began to tell her more about him and compare him with you.'"

"'Well?' says he."

"'Well, she got into a temper, and told me that she would not allow Mr. Blake's name to be associated with yours in her room.'"

"Then, sur, that 'ere willain he swore like a trooper, and said he'd make you rue the day you were born. After that, they were silent for a little while, and then she says to him—

"'I believe she knows what you are wanting to do, and has some idea of the influence you have exerted over him. She's as sharp as a lancet, and it's difficult to deceive her.'"

"'If only that Blake hadn't come,' he says, as if talkin' to hisself."

"'Yes,' she says, 'but he has come,' says she."

"'But if he can be made to leave her, and never speak to her again, will it not show to her that he's what you said he was, and thus turn her against him?'

"'I don't know. She's been cool enough to drive him away,' said that 'ere Miss Staggles."

"'But if he leaves disgraced, proved to be a villain, a deceiver, a blackleg, or worse than that, while I show up as an angel of light?'"

"'I don't know,' she says. 'You are a wonderful man; you can do almost anything. You could charm even an angel.'"

"'Well, you'll do your best for me, won't you?' says he."

"'You know I will,' she says; 'but we must not be seen together like this, or they will suspect something.'"

"'True,' says he, 'but I want to know how things are goin' on.' Then he stopped a minit, and a thought seemed to strike him. 'Miss Staggles, my friend,' he says, 'watch her closely, and meet me here on New Year's Day, at five o'clock in the evening. It's dark then, and everybody will be indoors.'"

"Then, yer honour, they went away together, and I was on the look-out for you all day yesterday."

There was much in Simon's story to think about, and for a time all was mystery to me. One thing, however, I thought was clear. He had either found he could do no good by his mesmeric influences, or else he had lost them, and so he was working up some other scheme against me. I pondered long over the words, "If he leaves disgraced, proved to be a villain, a deceiver, a blackleg, or worse than that, while I show up as an angel of light?" Surely that meant a great deal! I must be on the watch. I must be as cunning as he. I did not like eavesdropping or playing the spy, and yet I felt there were times when it would be right to do so, and surely that time had come in my history. There was villainy to be unmasked, there was a true, innocent girl to be saved, while my reputation, happiness, and perhaps life were in danger. I determined I would meet stratagem with stratagem. I would hear this conference in the wood that evening. I would seek to undeceive Miss Forrest, too, whose behaviour was now explained. Accordingly, after a few more words with Simon, I wended my way back to the house again.

I found Miss Forrest still in the library, together with Tom Temple and Edith Gray. All three looked up brightly at my entrance.

"We were just talking about you, Justin," said Tom, as I joined them. "I had been telling these ladies what a terrible woman-avoider you have always been. Miss Forrest wouldn't believe me at first; but that story of your walking five miles alone, rather than ride in a carriage with some ladies, has convinced her. I thought you had improved the first day or so after you came, but you seem to have fallen back into your old ways."

"Don't put the fault on me, Tom," I said.

"The fault has generally been with the ladies. The truth is, I'm not a ladies' man, and hence not liked by them. I have generally been put down as a kind of bore, I expect, and I've never taken the trouble to improve my reputation."

"Then you ought," said Miss Gray, laughingly. "It's a shame that you should be under such a ban, because if a man can't make himself pleasant to ladies, what *can* he do?"

"Well, I should like to turn over a new leaf," I replied; "but then I don't seem to please. I've no doubt my company is very tiring, and thus I must be left out in the cold."

"Nonsense," replied Tom. "Let us have another ride this afternoon, and see whether you can't make Miss Forrest a pleasant companion."

"If Miss Forrest would allow me, I should be delighted," I said.

I expected an excuse, such as a cold, a headache, or some previous engagement, especially as she had looked steadily into the fire while we had been talking. Instead of this, however, she frankly accepted my escort, and accordingly the ride was arranged.

Nothing of importance happened before we started. We had gone out quietly, and had attracted no notice, and rode away towards the ruins of an old castle which Tom thought we should like to visit.

As I stated, it was a raw, cold day; but I did not feel the biting wind, or notice the weird desolation that was all around. I felt supremely happy as I rode by Miss Forrest's side.

We had gone perhaps two miles from the house, when we found ourselves separated from Tom Temple and Miss Gray, and we slackened our horses' speed to a walk.

"Have you thought my conduct strange since we last rode out

together?" she said.

"I have indeed," I replied bluntly, "especially as I do not remember having done anything that should merit your evident dislike to me."

"I owe you an apology," she said. "I have been very foolish, very unjust. I am very sorry."

"But might I ask why you saw fit to change your conduct from friendliness to extreme aversion?"

"I'm almost ashamed to tell you, Mr. Blake, but I will. If there is one thing for which I have aversion and contempt, it is for flirting, coquetry, and the like. If there is any species of mankind that I despise, it is that of a flirt, a society man, a ladies' man."

"And have I ever given evidence of belonging to that class, Miss Forrest?"

"No," she replied; "and that is why I am so ashamed of myself. But I listened to some foolish gossip about your boasting of your conquests with ladies and the like. I know I ought not to have listened to it, but I did. I am very sorry; will you forgive me?"

She said this frankly, and without hesitation; yet I thought I saw a blush mount her cheek as she spoke.

"If there is anything to forgive, I do forgive you," I replied, "especially as I despise that class of individuals as much as you. The vapid, dancing society mannikin is everywhere an object of contempt, while a society girl, as generally accepted, is not a whit more to my taste."

I saw she was pleased at this, and I felt I loved her more than ever. Did she, I wondered, care anything for me? Was there any vestige of interest in her heart beyond that which she felt for any passing acquaintance?

"Mr. Blake," she said, after pausing a second, "do you remember what we were talking about that day when we last rode out together?"

"We were talking of Mr. Voltaire," I said. "Have you found out anything more about him?"

"No, I have not. Is there any mystery connected with him?"

"I think there is. I have an indistinct kind of feeling that both he and the Egyptian are deceivers, while I am sure that Mr. Voltaire is—is your enemy."

"I have no doubt he is," I said.

She looked at me strangely.

"I had not been in Temple Hall two hours before that man had marked me as one that he would fain be rid of."

"Indeed," she said; "then if that is the case, you should listen to my advice. Have nothing to do with him."

"But I must have something to do with him, and with his friend the Egyptian as well."

"Don't," she said anxiously; "the two work together, and both are cunning as serpents. I believe," she continued, after a pause, "that the thought-reading and mesmerism were somehow designed to injure you. I think somehow they are acquainted with forces unknown to us, and will use them for evil."

"Yes, I believe all that," I said.

"Then why must you have any dealings with them?"

"Because they will have dealings with me; because they are plotting against me; because there are forces, over which I have no control, drawing me on."

"But why will they have dealings with you? Why are they plotting against you?"

"Because Voltaire knows that I love, with all my soul, the woman he wants to win for his wife."

A curious look shot across her face. What was it? Love, astonishment, pain, vexation, or joy? I could not tell; but my tongue was unloosed.

"Do I annoy you, astonish you, Miss Forrest?" I said. "Forgive me if I do. I have been regarded as a woman-hater, a society-avoider. That is because I never saw a woman in whom I was sufficiently interested to court her society. I have heard it said that such characters fall in love quickly, or not at all. The first day I saw you I fell in love with you; I love you now with all my soul."

She looked at my face steadily, but did not speak a word.

"Voltaire has found out this, and he too wants you for his wife; so he has been trying—is trying—to drive me away from here. How I cannot tell you; but what I have said is true!" I spoke rapidly, passionately, and I saw that her face became alternately pale and red, but she did not reply.

"Am I bold to speak thus?" I asked. "I think I must be, for I have scarcely known you a week. But I cannot help it. My life is given up to you. If I could but know that my love were not in vain! If you could give me some word of hope!"

A beautiful look lit up her eyes; she opened her mouth to speak, when a voice shouted—

"Come, Justin; don't loiter so. We shall not get back in time for dinner, if you do."

It was Tom Temple who spoke, and a turn in the lane revealed him. To say I was sorry would be but to hint at my feelings. But I could not hinder the turn things had taken, so we started our horses into a gallop, I hoping that soon another opportunity might occur for our being alone, when I trusted she would tell me what I desired to know.

I do not know how I dared to make my confession of love, for certainly I had but little proof of her caring for me. If I hoped, it was almost without reason; and yet, as we galloped on, my heart beat right joyfully.

Nothing of importance occurred during the ride. The castle we visited was grim and grey enough; but it was not the kind of afternoon when one could enjoy to the full such a place, so we were not long before we turned our horses' heads homeward. Time after time, on our homeward journey, did I contrive to be alone with Miss Forrest, but always in vain. She kept by the side of Edith Gray in spite of all my schemes to get her by mine. Her lips were compressed, and her eyes had a strange look. I longed to know what she was thinking about, but her face revealed nothing.

We came to the house at length, however, and then I hastened from her side to lift her from the saddle. Then my heart gave a great throb, for I thought she returned the pressure of my hand.

Joseph Hocking

"Do be careful about that man," she said hurriedly, and then ran into the house.

It was joy and light to me, and I needed it in the dark days that came after.

The stable-boy had scarcely taken the horses when a thought struck me. I looked at my watch, and it was almost too dark for me to discern the time, but I saw, after some difficulty, that it wanted but a few minutes to five. In my joy I had forgotten my determination, but now I quickly made my way to the summer-house that stood in the dark fir plantation.

CHAPTER IX

THE HALL GHOST

Perhaps some of my readers may think I was doing wrong in determining to listen to the proposed conference between Miss Staggles and Voltaire. I do not offer any excuse, however. I felt that if this man was to be fought, it must be by his own weapons; such, at any rate, as I could use. I remembered the terrible influence he had exercised over me, the power of which might not yet be broken. I remembered Miss Forrest too. Evidently this man was a villain, and wanted to make her his wife. To stop such an event, I would devote my life. Something important might be the result of such a conversation. I might hear disclosed the secret of his influence, and thereby discover the means whereby I could be free, and this freedom might, I hoped, make me his master.

Anyhow, I went. The dark clouds which swept across the sky hid the pale rays of the moon, and, clothed in black as I was, it would be difficult to see me amongst the dark tall trees. I hurried to the summer-house, for I wished to be there before they arrived. I was successful in this. When I came, all was silent; so I got behind a large tree, which, while it hid me from any one entering the house, enabled me to be within earshot of anything that might be said, especially so as the

Joseph Hocking

summer-house was a rustic affair, and the sides by no means thick.

Silently I waited for, I should think, half-an-hour; then a woman came alone. Evidently she was cold, for she stamped her feet against the wood floor with great vehemence. Minute after minute passed by, and still there was no third party. Then I heard a low "hist."

"You're late," said the woman's voice, which I recognized as Miss Staggles'."

"Yes; and we must not stay long."

"Why?"

"Because I think we are watched."

"But why should we be watched? Surely no one perceives that we are suspicious parties?"

"I cannot say. I only know I cannot stay long."

"Why, again?"

"I have much to think about, much to do." "And I have much to tell you."

"I can guess it, I think; but I must know. Tell me quickly."

He spoke peremptorily, as if he had a right to command, while she did not resent his dictatorial tones.

"They've been riding together again to-day."

"I guessed it. Bah! what a fool I've been! But there, that may mean nothing."

"But it does; it means a great deal."

"What?"

"I believe that he's asked her to be his wife. In fact, I'm sure he has."

"Darkness and death, he has! And she?"

"I hardly know; but as sure as we are alive, she likes him."

"How do you know this?"

"I saw them come in from their ride, and so I guessed that they had become friendly again."

"Well?"

"Well, I met her in the hall. She looked as happy as a girl could well look. I am a woman, so I began to put two and two together. I determined to listen. I went up-stairs to my room, which, you know, is close to Miss Gray's and Gertrude's. If you had known girls as long as I, you would know that they usually make friends and confidantes of each other. I found this to be true in the present case. Gertrude had not been in their room above five minutes before Miss Gray came to the door and asked to come in. It was immediately opened, and she entered."

"And what then?"

"I listened."

"Just so; I expected that. But what did you hear?"

"I could not catch all they said; but I gathered that they had a delightful ride, that Mr. Blake had made a declaration of love to Gertrude."

"And her answer?"

"I could not catch that; she spoke too low. But I should think it was favourable, for there was a great deal of whispering, and after a while I heard something about that dreadful man being Mr. Blake's enemy."

"Ah! How did they know that?"

"I gathered that Mr. Blake told her. Look here, Herod Voltaire; you are playing a losing game."

"I playing a losing game? Do not fear. I'll win, I'll win, or— or—" Here he paused, as if a thought struck him.

"Why don't you get an influence over her, as you did over Blake? Then you could manage easily." "I cannot. I've tried; her nature is not susceptible; besides, even if I got such a power, I could not use it. You cannot force love, and the very nature of the case would make such a thing impossible. Stay! You know Miss Forrest well, don't you, her education, and her disposition?"

"I've known her long enough."

"Well, tell me whether I am correct in my estimate of her character. If I am, I do not fear. She's very clear-headed, sharp, and clever; a hater of humbug, a despiser of cant."

"True enough; but what's this got to do with the matter?"

"In spite of this, however," went on Voltaire without heeding

Miss Staggles' query, "she has a great deal of romance in her nature; has a strong love for mystery, so much so that she is in some things a trifle superstitious."

"I can't say as to that, but I should think you are correct."

"Then she's a young lady of very strong likes and dislikes, but at bottom is of a very affectionate nature."

"Affectionate to nearly every one but me," muttered Miss Staggles.

"She is intensely proud—"

"As Lucifer!" interrupted Miss Staggles. "This is her great weakness," went on Voltaire. "Her pride will overcome her judgment, and because of it she will do things for which she will afterwards be sorry. Is this true?"

"True to the letter. You must be a wizard, Herod Voltaire, or you couldn't have summed up her disposition so correctly."

"Her sense of honour is very great. She would sacrifice her happiness to do what was thought to be honourable."

"I believe she would."

"Then my path is marked out," said he, savagely.

From that time I could catch nothing of what was said, although they conversed for five minutes at least. But it was in whispers, so low that I could not catch a word.

Presently they got up and went away, while I, with aching head and fast-beating heart, tried to think what to do. Everything was mystery. I could not see a step before me.

Joseph Hocking

Why should Miss Staggles be so willing to help Herod Voltaire, and what were the designs in his mind? What was his purpose in getting at a correct estimate of Miss Forrest's character?

I went to the house pondering these things in my mind, and, arriving there, heard the hall clock strike the quarter, from which I knew it was a quarter past six. We were to dine at seven that day, and, as I did not usually make an elaborate toilette, I knew I had plenty of time. I felt I could not go in for a few minutes; my brain seemed on fire. I turned to take a walk towards the park gates, when I heard a footstep, and turning, saw Simon Slowden.

"Can you give me ten minutes before dinner, sur?" he said.

"I dare say," I said.

He led me into the room in which we had spoken together before. "There's something wrong, yer honour," he said in a low voice.

"How do you know?"

"Why, that 'ere Egyptian hev bin doggin' me all day. He's got a hinklin' as how we're tryin' to match 'em, and reckons as how I'm yer friend. Besides, to-day when I see you ride hoff with the young lady, I thinks to myself, 'There's no knowin' what time he'll be back.' I know what 'tis, yer honour; hi've bin in the arms o' Wenus myself, and knows as 'ow a hour slips away like a minnit. So as there wur no tellin' if you would get to the summer-house to-night at five o'clock, I thought I'd just toddle up myself. But 'twas no go. I sees they two willains a-talkin' together, and when that 'ere Woltaire went off by himself, the other took it 'pon him to keep wi' me. I tried to git 'im off, but 'twas no use; he stuck to me like a limpet to a rock."

"Perhaps it was all fancy, Simon."

"No fancy in me, but a lot o' judgment. Fact, sur, I've begun to think for the fust time as 'ow some things in the Bible ain't true. In the Psalms of Solomon it reads, 'Resist the devil and he'll go away howlin'.' Well, I've resisted that 'ere devil, and he wouldn't go away till he'd knowed as how he'd played his little game;" and Simon looked very solemn indeed.

"Is that all, Simon?"

"All, yer honour. 'Tisn't much, you think; but to me it looks mighty suspicious, as I said to my sweetheart when I see her a-huggin' and kissin' the coachman."

I went away laughing, but my heart was still heavy. Try as I would, I could not dispel the fancy that soon something terrible would happen.

During dinner Kaffar made himself very disagreeable. This was somewhat unusual, as he was generally very bland and polite, but to-night he was so cantankerous that I fancied he must have been drinking. To me he was especially insulting, and went so far as to hint that I, unlike other Englishmen, was a coward; that I hadn't courage to resist a man manfully, but would act towards an enemy in a cunning, serpent-like way. This was not the first occasion on which he had sought to pick a quarrel with me, and I felt like resenting it. I desisted, however, as there were ladies present, and went on quietly talking to my neighbour as if he hadn't spoken. This roused his ire more, while I saw that Voltaire watched me with his light glittering eye, as if expecting a scene.

After dinner, this being New Year's Day, we passed a more

than usually merry time. Stories were told, old ballads were sung, while Roger de Coverley was danced in downright earnest by most of those who were present. By midnight, however, the old hall was silent; each of us had repaired to his room, and most, I expect, were quietly asleep, when a terrible scream was heard, after which there were shouts for help and hysterical cries. The sounds seemed to come from the direction of the servants' hall, and, quickly putting on some clothes, I hurried thither. I soon found that the noise had roused the whole household, and so, when I arrived, I found a number of the guests had gathered together. On looking into the room, I saw that the housekeeper was lying in a swoon, one of the servants was in hysterics, while Simon Slowden, who was in the room, and the page boy looked as white as sheets, and were trembling evidently with fear.

"What does this mean?" asked Tom Temple, a little angrily.

At this the housekeeper became conscious and said in a hoarse whisper, "Is she gone?"

"What? Who do you mean?" asked Tom.

"The hall lady," she said fearfully.

"We are all friends here," said Tom, and I thought I detected an amount of anxiety in his voice.

This appeared to assure the housekeeper, who got up and tried to collect her thoughts. We all waited anxiously for her to speak.

"I have stayed up late, Mr. Temple," she said to Tom, "in order to arrange somewhat for the party you propose giving on Thursday. The work had got behind, and so I asked two or three of the servants to assist me."

She stopped here, as if at a loss how to proceed.

"Go on, Mrs. Richards; we want to know all. Surely there must be something terrible to cause you all to arouse us in this way."

"I'll tell you as well as I can," said the housekeeper, "but I can hardly bear to think about it. Twas about one o'clock, and we were all very busy, when we heard a noise in the corridor outside the door. Naturally we turned to look, when the door opened and something entered."

"Well, what? Some servant walking in her sleep?"

"No, sir," said Mrs. Richards in awful tones. "It looked like a woman, very tall, and she had a long white shroud around her, and on it were spots of blood. In her hand she carried a long knife, which was also covered with blood, while the hand which held it was red. She came closer to us," she went on with a shudder, "and then stopped, lifting the terrible knife in the air. I cannot remember any more, for I was so terribly frightened. I gave an awful scream, and then I suppose I fainted."

This story was told with many interruptions, many pauses, many cries, and I saw that the faces of those around were blanched with fear.

"Do you know what it did, Simon," said Tom, turning to that worthy, "after it lifted its knife in the air?"

"She went away with a wail like," said Simon, slowly; "she opened the door and went out. An' then I tried to go to the door, and when I got there, there was nothin'."

"That is, you looked into the passage?"

Simon nodded. "And what did you think she was like?"

"Like the hall ghost, as I've heard so much about," said Simon.

"The hall ghost!" cried the ladies, hysterically. "What does that mean, Mr. Temple?"

I do not think Tom should have encouraged their superstition by telling them, but he did. He was excited, and scarcely knew what was best to do.

"They say that, like other old houses, Temple Hall has its ghost," he said; "that she usually appears on New Year's night. If the year is to be good to those within at the time, she comes with flowers and dressed in gay attire; if bad, she is clothed in black; if there's to be death for any one, she wears a shroud. But it's all nonsense, you know," said Tom, uneasily.

"And she's come in a shroud," said the servant who had been in hysterics, "and there was spots of blood upon it, and that means that the one who dies will be murdered; and there was a knife in her hand, and that means that 'twill be done by a knife."

It would be impossible to describe the effect this girl's words made. She made the ghost very real to many, and the calamity which she was supposed to foretell seemed certain to come to pass. I looked at Gertrude Forrest and Ethel Gray, who, wrapped in their dressing-gowns, stood side by side, and I saw that both of them were terribly moved.

Voltaire and Kaffar were both there, but they uttered no word. They, too, seemed to believe in the reality of the apparition.

After a great deal of questioning on the part of the lady guests, and many soothing replies on the part of the men, something like quietness was at length restored, and many of the braver ones began to return to their rooms, until Tom and I were left alone in the servants' hall. We again questioned the servants, but with the same result, and then we went quietly up-stairs. Arriving at the landing, we saw Miss Forrest and Miss Gray leaving Mrs. Temple at the door of her room. Tom hurried to Miss Gray, and took her by the hand, while I, nothing loth, spoke to Miss Forrest.

"There's surely some trick in this," I said to her.

I felt her hand tremble in mine as she spoke. "I do not know. It seems terribly real, and I have heard of such strange things."

"But you are not afraid? If you are, I shall be up all night, and will be so happy to help you."

I thought I felt a gentle pressure of her hand, but I was not sure; but I know that her look made me very happy as she, together with Edith Gray, entered her room a few minutes after.

When they had gone, I said to Tom, "I am not going to bed to-night."

"No?" said Tom. "Well, I'll stay up with you."

"This ghost affair is nonsense, Tom. I hope you will not find any valuables gone to-morrow."

"Real or not," said Tom, gaily, "I'm glad it came."

"How's that?"

Joseph Hocking

"It gave me nerve to pop the question," he replied. "I told my little girl just now—for she is mine now—that she wanted a strong man to protect such a weak little darling."

"And she?"

"She said that she knew of no one, whom she liked, that cared enough for her to protect her. So I told her I did, and then—well, what followed was perfectly satisfactory."

I congratulated him on his audacity, and then we spent the night in wandering about the first floor of the house, trying to find the ghost, but in vain; and when the morning came, and we all tried to laugh at the ghost, I felt that there was a deep, sinister meaning in it all, and wondered what the end would be.

CHAPTER X

THE COMING OF THE NIGHT

Directly after breakfast I went away alone. I wanted to get rid of an awful weight which oppressed me. I walked rapidly, for the morning was cold. I had scarcely reached the park gates, however, when a hand touched me. I turned and saw Kaffar.

"I hope your solitary walk is pleasant," he said, revealing his white teeth.

"Thank you," I replied coldly.

I thought he was going to leave me, but he kept close by my side, as if he wanted to say something. I did not encourage him to speak, however; I walked rapidly on in silence.

"Temple Hall is a curious place," he said.

"Very," I replied.

"So different from Egypt—ah, so different. There the skies are bright, the trees are always green. There the golden sandhills stretch away, the palm trees wave, the Nile sweeps majestic. There the cold winds scarcely ever blow, and the people's hearts are warm."

"I suppose so."

"There are mysteries there, as in Temple Hall, Mr. Blake; but mysteries are sometimes of human origin."

As he said this, he leered up into my face, as if to read my thoughts; but I governed my features pretty well, and thus, I think, deceived him.

"Perhaps you know this?" he said.

"No," I replied. "I am connected with no mysteries."

"Not with the appearance of the ghost last night?"

I looked at him in astonishment. The insinuation was so far from true that for the moment I was too surprised to speak.

He gave a fierce savage laugh, and clapped his hands close against my face. "I knew I was right," he said; and then, before I had time to reply, he turned on his heel and walked away.

Things were indeed taking curious turns, and I wondered what would happen next. What motive, I asked, could Kaffar have in connecting me with the ghost, and what was the plot which was being concocted? There in the broad daylight the apparition seemed very unreal. The servants, alone in the hall at midnight, perhaps talking about the traditional ghost, could easily have frightened themselves into the belief that they had seen it. Or perhaps one of their fellow-servants sought to play them a trick, and ran away when they saw what they had done. I would sift a little deeper. I immediately retraced my steps to the house, where meeting

Tom, I asked him to let me have Simon Slowden and a couple of dogs, as I wanted to shoot a few rabbits. This was easily arranged, and soon after Simon and I were together. Away on the open moors there was no fear of eavesdroppers; no one could hear what we said.

"Simon," I said, after some time, "have you thought any more of the wonderful ghost that you saw last night?"

Instantly his face turned pale, and he shuddered as if in fear. At any rate, the ghost was real to him.

"Yer honour," he said, "I don't feel as if I can talk about her. I've played in 'Amlet, yer honour, along with Octavius Bumpus's travellin' theatre, and I can nail a made-up livin' ghost in a minnit; but this ghost didn't look made up. There was no blood, yer honour; she looked as if she 'ad bin waccinated forty times."

"And were the movements of her legs and arms natural?"

"No j'ints, Master Blake. She looked like a wooden figger without proper j'ints! Perhaps she 'ad a few wire pins in her 'natomy; but no j'ints proper."

"So you believe in this ghost?"

"Can't help it, yer honour."

"Simon, I don't. There's some deep-laid scheme on foot somewhere; and I think I can guess who's working it."

Simon started. "You don't think that 'ere waccinatin', sumnamblifyin' willain 'ev got the thing in 'and?"

I didn't speak, but looked keenly at him.

At first he did nothing but stare vacantly, but presently a look of intelligence flashed into his eyes. Then he gave a shrug, as if he was disgusted with himself, which was followed by an expression of grim determination.

"Master Blake," he said solemnly, "it's that waccinatin' process as hev done it. Simon Slowden couldn't hev bin sich a nincompoop if he hadn't bin waccinated 'gainst whoopin' cough, measles, and small-pox. Yer honour," he continued, "after I wur waccinated I broke out in a kind of rash all over, and that 'ere rash must have robbed me of my senses; but I'm blowed—There, I can't say fairer nor that."

"Why, what do you think?"

"I daren't tell you, yer honour, for fear I'll make another mistake. I thowt, sur, as it would take a hangel with black wings to nick me like this 'ere, and now I've bin done by somebody; but it's the waccinatin', yer honour—it's the waccination. In the Proverbs of Job we read, 'fool and his money soon parted,' and so we can see 'ow true the teachin' is to-day."

"But what is to be done, Simon?"

Simon shook his head, and then said solemnly, "I'm away from my bearin's, sur. I thought when I wur done the last time it should be the last time. It wur in this way, sur. I was in the doctor's service as waccinated me. Says he, when he'd done, 'Simon, you'll never have small-pox now.' 'Think not?' says I. 'Never,' says he; and when Susan the 'ousemaid heard on it, she says, 'I am so glad, Simon.' Then, says I, 'Susan, when people are married they're converted into one flesh. That's scripter. You get married to me,' says I, 'and you'll be kept free from small-pox, without goin' threw this yer willifyin' process.' Wi' that she looks at me, and she says,

'You are purty, and I'll try you for three months; if you don't get small-pox in that time, why then—we'll talk about it.' So I says, 'Say yes at once, Susan. The doctor says I can't get it, so there's no sort o' fear.' I wur young and simple then, and thowt doctors never made a mistake. Well, sur, in two months more I were down wi' small-pox, and when I got up again I wur a sight to behold. As soon as I wur fit to be seen I went to Susan to git a mite o' comfort, and then I see 'er a-courtin' wi' the coachman. And I says to myself, 'Simon Slowden,' I says, 'this yer is the last time you must be ever taken in;' and now I'm right mad that I should 'a bin licked in this yer way."

I could not help laughing at Simon's story, in spite of my heavy heart, and so I asked him what the doctor said when he found vaccination a failure.

"Sent me off without a character, sur," he replied grimly. "Said he couldn't keep a servant as would be a livin' advertisement as 'ow his pet 'obby wer a failure. And so I allays say as 'ow vaccination is my ruin. It's ruined my blood and weakened my brain. Still," continued Simon, with a sly look, "I reckon as 'ow I'll be a match for that 'ere doubly vaccinated ghost as frightened me so."

I could get nothing more from him. He had formed some notion about the apparition which he would not divulge, so we devoted our attention to sport, and, after frightening a good many rabbits, we returned to the hall.

Nothing of importance happened through the day, except an inquiry which Tom made among the servants. Each declared that they were entirely ignorant as to the appearance of the ghost, and all were evidently too frightened to doubt the truth of their statement. Thus when evening came nothing was known of it.

Joseph Hocking

Kaffar did not speak to me from the time I had seen him in the morning to dinner-time, and evidently avoided me. Voltaire, on the contrary, was unusually bland and smiling. He was pleasant and agreeable to every one, especially so to me.

After dinner we all found our way to the drawing-room, when the usual singing, flirting, and dancing programme was carried out. Suddenly, however, there was comparative silence. One voice only was heard, and that was the Egyptian's.

"Yes," he was saying, "I am what is called a superstitious man. I believe in dreams, visions, and returned spirits of the dead. But, ah! I do not believe in made-up ghosts. Oh, you cold-blooded English people, don't mistake the impulsive Egyptian; don't accuse him of lack of faith in the unseen. So much do I believe in it, that sometimes I long to be with those who have gone. But, bah! the ghost last night was to deceive, to frighten. Got up by some villain for a purpose, and I can guess who he is."

"This is serious," said Tom Temple. "I have inquired of the servants, who all assure me of their entire ignorance of the matter, and I cannot think that any of my guests would assume the person of the traditional ghost for no other purpose than to frighten the housekeeper and two or three servants. I'm by no means superstitious, but I do not see how I can trace it to human origin."

"I cannot see why any guest should assume the person of the traditional ghost, but some men have deep designing minds. They are like clever draught-players; they see half-a-dozen moves ahead, and so do that which to a novice appears meaningless and absurd."

Then I heard another voice, one that caused my heart to beat wildly. It was Gertrude Forrest's. "Mr. Kaffar says he can guess who the person is who has personated this ghost," she said; "I think it fair to every guest that he should speak out."

"I would not like to say," he said insultingly; "perchance I should wound *your* tender feelings too deeply."

"Mr. Kaffar will remember he's speaking to a lady, I'm sure," said Tom Temple.

"Pardon me," said Kaffar, excitedly; "I forgot I was in England, where men are the slaves of the ladies. With us it is different. We speak and they obey. I forgot I was not in Egypt. I have done very wrong. I implore the lady's pardon."

"I see no meaning in your words," said Miss Forrest, quietly, "therefore I see nothing to forgive."

"Ah, I live again. A heavy load is gone from my heart! I have not merited the lady's displeasure."

"Still I think it right, if you have grounds for suspecting any one, that we should know," said a voice; "otherwise some one may be wrongly accused."

"Do not ask me," said Kaffar. "Ask Mr. Blake."

Instantly all eyes were turned on me, and, do as I might, I could not help an uncomfortable flush rising in my face. "I do not know what Mr. Kaffar means," I replied. "I am as ignorant as to the origin of the ghost as he is, perhaps more so."

Instantly Kaffar leapt from his chair, and came up to me, his hands clenched, his black eyes gleaming, his teeth set together as if in a terrible rage.

"You are a liar and a villain!" he screamed.

"Ah, remember this morning. I accused him, gentlemen, of being connected with this ghost only to-day, and he flushed guiltily and was silent. He looked like a Judas who betrayed his master."

"Quietly, please," I replied. "You did come to me this morning with some foolish jargon about my being connected with last night's affair, but I was so surprised by the absurdity and foolishness of such a thing, that I could not answer you before you ran away."

"You hear?" shrieked the Egyptian. "So surprised, was he? If he was, it was because I had found him out."

"This man is mad," I said. "Surely he ought to be shut up."

"Mad, am I?" he shrieked. "Yes, and you are a liar, a coward, a villain! You are engaged in a fiendish plot; you are deceiving an innocent lady. Ah, I spurn you, spit upon you."

"Mr. Kaffar," said Tom Temple, "really this cannot be allowed. You must remember you are among gentlemen and ladies. Please act accordingly."

"Ladies there are, gentlemen there are," shrieked the Egyptian; "but he"—pointing at me—"is no gentleman. He is at once a viper, a villain, and a coward. I leave this house; I renounce pleasant society; I leave this country—for ever; but before I go I would like to fight hand to hand with that giant, who—Ha!" He stood close to me and spat at me. "There!" he cried, and then he struck me in the face with all his strength.

Instantly I leapt to my feet. This insult was too great. I could scarcely restrain from striking him to the ground. I mastered myself, however, and so did not touch him.

"I leave this house," he said wildly. "Herod, send on my baggage to Cairo. But"—turning to me—"you I challenge— you, with your big body and trained arms! But, bah! you dar'n't fight. You are a mooning coward."

He rushed out of the room as he spoke, and a minute later I heard the hall door slammed with vehemence.

At that moment I became possessed of a terrible passion. I seemed to be mad. I longed to avenge the insults that had been offered. I looked around the room, and all seemed astounded at the behaviour of the Egyptian, save Voltaire, who was apologizing in profuse terms for his friend. As I looked at his terrible eyes, my passion became greater, and I felt I could not govern myself if I stayed in the room. I think some one came up to me, and congratulated me on my coolness in dealing with the man who had insulted me so; but I did not listen—I could not. An overmastering impulse laid hold of me to follow the Egyptian, and I dimly remember going into the hall and out into the silent night.

I knew the probability was that I should be followed, but I did not know where to go, when I seemed to hear voices all around me uttering the words "Drearwater Pond!" With that I started running with all my might, knowing not where, yet dimly remembering that I had gone the road before. Then all memory and consciousness ceased.

Joseph Hocking

CHAPTER XI

DARK DREAMS AND NIGHT SHADOWS

I suppose I must have gone on blindly for some time, for when I again became conscious I stood beside a river, while tall trees waved their leafless branches overhead. Strange noises filled the air. Sometimes wailing sounds were wafted to me, which presently changed into hisses, until it seemed as if a thousand serpents were creeping all around me. The waters of the river looked black, while above me were weird, fantastic forms leaping in the stillness of the night. No words were spoken, no language was uttered, save that of wailing and hissing, and that somehow was indistinct, as if it existed in fancy and not in reality. By and by, however, I heard a voice.

"Onward!" it said, and I became unconscious.

*   *   *   *   *

Again I realized my existence in a vague shadowy way. I stood beneath the ruined walls of an Eastern temple. Huge columns arose in the air, surmounted by colossal architraves, while the ponderous stones of which the temple was built were covered with lichen. Large grey lizards crawled in and out among the crevices of the rocks, and seemed to laugh as they sported amidst what was once the expression of a great religious system, but which was now terrible in its weird desolation. By and by the great building seemed to assume its original shape and became inhabited by white-robed priests, who ministered to the people who came to worship. I watched eagerly, but they faded away, leaving nothing save the feeling that a terrible presence filled the place. I heard a noise behind; I turned and saw Kaffar, his black eyes shining, while in his hand he held a gleaming knife. He lifted it above his head as if to strike; but I had the strength of ten men, and I hurled him from me. He looked at me with a savage leer.

"Onward!" said a distant voice.

The temple vanished, and with it all my realization of life, save a vague fancy that I was moving somewhere, I knew not where.

*   *   *   *   *

I stood by a well-remembered spot. I was by the side of Drearwater Pond. Around me was a stretch of common land, on which grew heather and furze. In front of me were noiseless waters, a dismal sight at the best of times, but awful as I saw them. Across the pond in the near distance loomed the dark fir trees. No sound broke the stillness of the night. The wind had gone to rest, the moon shone dimly from behind the misty clouds.

I stood alone.

Each minute my surroundings became more real. I recognized more clearly the objects which had struck me during my first visit, while the stories which had been told came back to me with terrible distinctness. I remembered how it had been said that the pond had no bottom, and that it was haunted by the spirits of those that had been murdered. The story of its evil influence came back to me, and in my bewildered condition I wondered whether there was not some truth in what had been said.

What was that?

The waters moved; distinctly moved near to where I stood, and from their dark depths something appeared—I could not at first tell what.

What could it be? A monster of frightful mien? the ghost of some murdered man or woman? I could have believed in either just then. It was neither.

What then? A human hand, large and shapely, appeared distinctly on the surface of the pond. Nothing more, not even the wrist to which it might be attached. It did not beckon, or indeed move at all; it was as still as the hand of death.

I stood motionless and watched, while the outline of the hand became more clear; then I gave an awful shudder.

The hand was red.

I gave a shriek, and for a time remembered nothing more.

*   *   *   *   *

I awoke to consciousness, fighting. At first it seemed as if I was fighting with a phantom, but gradually my opponent became more real to me. It was Kaffar.

I had only a dim hazy idea of what I was doing, except that I sought to wrest from his hand a knife. We clutched each other savagely, and wrestled there on the edge of the pond. Weights seemed to hang upon my limbs, but I felt the stronger of the two. Gradually I knew I was mastering him—then all was blank.

*   *   *   *   *

A sound of voices. A flash of light. A feeling of freedom, and I was awake!

Where?

Still by Drearwater Pond. No phantoms, no shadow, nothing unreal, save the memory of that which I have but dimly described. That was but as a terrible nightmare—an awful dream.

Where was Kaffar?

I could not tell. Certainly he was not near; but two other forms stood by me, one bearing a lantern.

"Is it you, Justin?" said a voice.

"It is I, Tom," I said, looking vacantly around.

"And where is Kaffar?" said another voice, which I recognized as Voltaire's.

"Kaffar? I—I do not know."

"But you have been together."

"Have we?" I said vacantly.

"You know you have. What is that in your hand?"

I had scarcely known what I had been saying or doing up to this time, but as he spoke I looked at my hand.

In the light of the moon I saw a knife red with blood, and my hand, too, was also discoloured.

"What does this mean?" cried Voltaire.

"I do not know. I am dazed—bewildered."

"But that is Kaffar's knife. I know he had it this very evening. Where is Kaffar now?"

"Is it true?" I remember saying. "Have we been together?" "That's his knife, at any rate. And what is this?"

Voltaire picked up something from the ground and looked at it. "Kaffar's," he said. "Look, Mr. Blake; do you recognize this?"

I looked and saw a finely-worked neckcloth, on which was written in Arabic characters the words "Aba Wady Kaffar." It had every appearance of being soiled by severe wrenching, and on it were spots of blood.

My faculties were rapidly returning to me, yet I stood as one in a dream.

"You say, Mr. Justin Blake, that you do not know where Kaffar is, yet you hold in your hand his knife, which is red with blood. Here is his scarf, which has evidently been strained, and on it are spots of blood, while all around are marks indicating a struggle. I say you do know what this means, and you must tell us."

I reeled under this terrible shock. What had I done? Could it be that I had murdered this man? Had I? Had I?

"I do not know what it means," I said. "I think I am ill."

"Men usually are when they have done what you have," he said.

"Why, what have I done?" I said, in a dazed kind of a way. "Done!" he repeated. "You know best about that, in spite of the part you play. Nevertheless, Kaffar has not gone without leaving a friend behind him, and you will have to show how you came by that"—pointing to the knife, which I had dropped with a shudder; "this"—holding up the neckcloth; "you must explain these marks"—pointing to footmarks near the water's edge; "besides which, you will have to produce my friend."

A terrible thought flashed into my mind. I had again been acting under the influence of this man's power. By some means he had made me the slave of his will, and I had unknowingly killed Kaffar, and he, like the fiend he was, had come to sweep me out of his road. Perchance, too, Kaffar's death might serve him in good stead. Undoubtedly the Egyptian knew too much for Voltaire, and so I was made a tool whereby he could be freed from troublesome obstacles. The idea maddened me. I would proclaim the story to every one. If I were hanged I cared not. I opened my mouth to tell Tom the whole truth, but I could not utter a word. My tongue refused to articulate; my power of speech left me.

My position was too terrible. My overwrought nerves yielded at last. I felt my head whirling around, while streams of icy water seemed to be running down my legs. Then I fell down at Tom Temple's feet.

For some time after that I remembered nothing distinctly. I

have some idea of stumbling along, with Tom on one side of me and Voltaire on the other, but no word was spoken until we came to Temple Hall. Then I heard Tom say—

"He's better now. You go into the drawing-room as if nothing had happened, and I'll take him quietly up-stairs to bed."

I entered the silent house like one in a dream, and went with Tom to my bedroom, where I undressed like a weary child, and soon sunk into a deep dreamless sleep.

CHAPTER XII

A MIDNIGHT CONFERENCE

Some one was knocking at the door.

"Who's there?"

"Tom Temple."

I sprang out of bed and let him in. He looked very grave, very worried. Instantly everything flashed through my mind in relation to our terrible meeting of the night before.

"It's nine o'clock, Justin."

"Yes, Tom, I suppose it must be," I said confusedly; "but I have only just awoke."

"I thought I must come; I want to talk with you."

"Thank you, Tom; I am glad you have come."

"How are you this morning? Is your mind clear?"

"Fairly. Why?"

"I must have some conversation with you about last night. Everything is confusion. I can explain nothing."

"Neither can I."

He looked at me keenly and sighed. "Were you with Kaffar last night after he had so abominably insulted you and left the house?"

"I do not know."

"Do you know where he is now?"

"No."

"No idea whatever?"

"Not the slightest."

"Justin, my friend, this looks very strange. Everything is terribly black, terribly suspicious."

I tried to tell him all I knew; tried to tell him of my mad passion, and the scenes through which I seemed to go; but I could not. My mind refused to think, my tongue refused to speak, when that was the subject.

"I suppose Voltaire has told every one the circumstances of last night?" I said at length.

"No."

"No one?"

"No one that will divulge anything. Every one else thinks that Kaffar has gone back to Egypt, as he said, and especially so as Voltaire has been making arrangements for his luggage to be sent to Cairo."

"This is astounding. I do not comprehend in the least; but, tell me, who is this some one to whom you or he has related last night's affair, and why was it done?"

"I do not know whether I ought to tell or no, but you are an old friend, and I cannot refuse. After I had come down from here last night, and fancying that every one had retired, for it was quite midnight, I, knowing I was too excited to sleep, made my way to the library. I had just reached the door when I heard voices. I wondered who could be up at that time of the night, but was not left to remain long in doubt."

"'Mr. Voltaire,' said a voice, 'you have been out looking for Mr. Blake; have you found him?'"

"'Mr. Blake is safe in bed before this, Miss Forrest— probably asleep,' was his reply."

"Miss Forrest!" I cried. "Did she go to him?"

"Evidently," replied Tom. "Indeed, I found out afterwards that she had been very anxious. She had seen you go out, and watched Voltaire and me, who went in search of you, and would not retire until she knew your whereabouts."

"Well, what then?"

"I went into the room. I could not stand and play the eavesdropper. Miss Forrest seemed very glad to see me, and said eagerly—

"'I came down to ask whether you had found Mr. Blake. I am glad he is safe.'"

"'And he must remain safe!' cried Voltaire."

"'Why?' asked Miss Forrest."

"'Miss Forrest,' cried Voltaire, vehemently, 'you have been deprived of your rest to-night in order to know about one who is guilty of what you English people call a foul crime, but which I call a deed that must be avenged.'"

"'I do not understand you.'"

"'Ah! Miss Forrest, we Easterns are not like you English people. You are cool and considerate; we are warm and impulsive. Kaffar was not one that could be loved by you cold people; but I loved him. We were more than brothers. I know he was faulty, I know he dared the anger of your English giant, but I did not think it would come to this.'"

"'Come to what?' she asked eagerly."

"'Voltaire,' I said, 'is this quite fair?'"

"'No, no!' he cried; 'but I am so excited that I can scarcely master myself. I will say no more.'"

"'Come to what?' repeated Miss Forrest."

"'I will not say,' replied Voltaire. 'I will not wound your tender nature; I will not tell you a tale of villainy; I will not cause a ripple on the even stream of your life. Retire to rest, sweet lady, and think that what I have said is a dream.'"

"'Villainy!' cried she. 'Tell me what it is. Yes, there is villainy, I think. I will be answered! Tell me the truth!'

"Even Voltaire was cowed by her words. He stood and

looked at her for a minute as if in doubt what to do. Then he burst out passionately—

"'Yes, I will answer you. I will tell you now what all the world must know to-morrow. I had hoped to spare your feelings, but the tone of your demand makes me speak.'"

"'He has no proof for what he is going to say,' I said."

"'Proof!' cried Voltaire. 'There is sufficient proof for an English court of law, and that law is terribly hard on murderers.'"

"'Murderers!' cried Miss Forrest. 'What do you mean?'"

"'This!' cried Voltaire. 'You saw Kaffar challenge Mr. Blake in the drawing-room?'"

"'I saw him insult Mr. Blake. I saw that Mr. Blake refrained from crushing him beneath his heel like a reptile. I saw that!' she cried excitedly.

"'Just so,' said Voltaire. 'Then Kaffar went out, and Mr. Blake went after him.'"

"'After him! Where?'"

"'Mr. Temple and I did not like the look on his face, and we followed him. I traced his footsteps along the high-road for a long while, and then we lost sight of them. We knew not where to go, when Mr. Temple thought he heard voices away in the distance. We went in the direction of the sound, and came to Drearwater Pond.'"

"'Drearwater Pond? That terrible place to which we rode the other day?'"

Joseph Hocking

"'The same, gentle lady.'"

"'And then?'"

"'When we came there we found Mr. Blake in a reclining position, with a bloody knife in his hand. I recognized it as belonging to Kaffar. I saw something lying on the ground, and, on picking it up, found it to be a scarf which Kaffar had been wearing this very night. It was twisted and soiled, and on it were spots of blood. Footmarks were to be seen on the edge of the deep pond, indicating a struggle; but Kaffar was nowhere to be seen.'"

"'It cannot be! It cannot be!' said Miss Forrest. 'But what then?'

"'I asked Mr. Blake questions. I accused him of many things, but he denied nothing.'"

"'Denied nothing?'"

"'Nothing, Miss Forrest. He tacitly admitted everything. I wish I could think otherwise; but oh, I am afraid my friend, my only friend, lies murdered at the bottom of Drearwater Pond, and murdered by Mr. Blake.'"

"'It cannot be!' cried Miss Forrest. 'Mr. Blake could never, *never* do so. There is some mistake.'"

"He took something from his pocket which was wrapped in a handkerchief. He removed this wrapping, and there revealed the knife you held in your hand.

"'This blood cries out for vengeance,' he said; 'ay, and it shall be avenged too.'"

"She gave a scream as if in pain. 'Why, what will you do?' she cried.

"'Were I in Egypt, my vengeance would be speedy,' he said, his light eyes glittering; 'but I am debarred from that here. Still, there is a means of vengeance. Your English law is stern. To-morrow the whole country shall shudder because of this dark deed, and to-morrow night that man, Justin Blake, shall sleep in a felon's cell'

"'No, no!' she cried. 'Not that. Have mercy.'"

"'Yes, yes!' he said, his voice husky with passion. 'What mercy did he have upon my friend? I will have vengeance, and my vengeance is just.'"

Try as I might, I could not help shuddering at this. A felon's cell! My name mentioned with loathing! 'Twas too horrible. I tried to conquer myself, however, and to tell Tom to go on with his recital. He continued—

"'Does any one know of these things besides you two?' she said at length."

"'No,' replied Voltaire. 'No one has had a chance of knowing.'"

Tom stopped in his recital, as if he would rather not tell what followed.

"What next, Tom?" I cried eagerly.

"I am thinking whether it is fair to her to tell you, and yet it is right you should know."

"What was it, Tom?"

She threw herself down on her knees before us, and besought us to keep the matter in our own hearts.

"'It is not true!' she cried; 'Mr. Blake would never do such a thing. There is some mistake. Promise me no word shall be uttered as to this. Mr. Kaffar has left, as he said, and gone back to Egypt. Why, then, should such a terrible suspicion be aroused? I will answer for Mr. Blake's innocence.'"

"'You answer, Miss Forrest?' cried Voltaire. 'Nay, you cannot. I would I could be merciful, but it must not be. My friend's spirit would haunt me from town to town and land to land.'"

"'Mr. Temple,' she cried to me, 'you will not tell, will you? You will not spread such a deceptive story about?'"

"'No,' I replied, 'I will not. Like you, I think there must be a mistake. My friend Justin could never do this.'"

"'There,' she cried to Voltaire; 'there's only you to be silent. Do it for my sake!'"

I could not help feeling a great throb of joy in my heart at this. I was sure now that she loved me. I could bear anything after hearing those words. I was happy in spite of the terrible net that was woven around me.

"'For your sake,' said Voltaire—'for your sake I could do almost anything. For your sake I could give up home, friends, happiness, life. Yes, I say this, here, in the presence of my friend Temple. I could forego anything for you. I would sacrifice father and mother for you.'"

I gave a great start.

"Justin, that man trembled like a leaf. His face became ashy pale; his terrible eyes became brighter than ever.

"'You ask me much,' he continued. 'You ask me to give up what is now the dearest object of my life—except one. But, ah! I am an Eastern. I am selfish; I cannot sacrifice disinterestedly. There is only one thing for which I can give up my scheme of vengeance.'"

"'Tell me what it is,' she cried."

"'Ah, sweet lady, I dare not tell; and yet I must. It is you. Be my wife, Miss Forrest; let me call you by your name, and I will wipe the blood from this knife, I will destroy every evidence of the dark deed. Justin Blake shall not lie in a prison cell; his name shall not be a synonym for devilry; he shall not be mentioned with loathing.'"

"And what then?" I cried. "What was her answer?"

"Man, she looked at him with loathing, but he did not see it."

"'Be your wife?' she said."

"'My wife, Miss Forrest,' he replied. 'Love cannot be greater than mine. I love the very ground on which you walk. Be my wife and I will be your slave. Your every desire shall be granted, and I will give up that which is dear to me.'"

"'And if I will not?' she said."

"'Ah, if you will not! Then—ah, I am an Eastern, and cannot give up everything. If I cannot have love, I must have vengeance.'"

"'But you have made a mistake. Your friend is alive. It is

absurd to think that Mr. Blake is guilty of such a deed.'"

"He pointed with a trembling hand to the bloody knife."

"'I can have no stronger proof than that,' he said, 'and that blood cries out for vengeance now.'"

"'Oh, I cannot,' she said, 'I cannot.'"

"'You refuse me?' he said quietly."

"'I must, I must,' she cried. 'It cannot be!'"

"He went to the writing-desk that stood near by, and commenced writing. 'If a poor Eastern cannot have love, he can still have vengeance,' he said.

"'What are you writing?' she cried."

"'I am writing a letter to the superintendent of the nearest police station, telling him to come with some men to Temple Hall to arrest a murderer.'"

"'Have you no mercy?' she said."

"'Mercy, lady. Only the Great Spirit above knows what I had made up my mind to give up, when I told you the condition on which I would be silent. I loved my friend as Jonathan loved David, and he is dead—murdered by an enemy's hand. Vengeance is one of the sweetest thoughts to an Eastern, and I meant to be avenged. You begged for his life, and I offered it—for your love. I asked you to marry me—me, who would give up everything for you; but you refused. I grieve for you, lady; but since I cannot have love, I must have revenge.'"

"He went on writing, while Miss Forrest clasped her hands as if in prayer."

"I am relating this very badly, Justin. I cannot remember many of the things that were said; I cannot call to mind all the gestures, the tones of voice, or the awful anguish which seemed to possess them both. I can only give you a scrappy account of what passed."

I remembered Tom's powers of memory, however, for which he had always been remarkable at school, and I knew that the account he gave me was not far from correct, and I begged him to go on.

"At length she turned to him again," continued Tom. "'I am going to show,' she said, 'that I believe Mr. Blake innocent. You asked me for love; that I cannot give you. I do not love you, I never shall love you; but such is my belief in Mr. Blake's innocence that I promise you this: if he is not proved to be guiltless within a year, I will marry you.'"

"He leapt to his feet, as if to embrace her."

"'No,' she said; 'you have not heard all my conditions. Within that year you are not to see me or communicate with me.'"

"'But,' he cried, 'if Kaffar is dead, if these terrible evidences of murder are real, then in a year—say next Christmas Eve; 'twas on Christmas Eve we first met in England—then you will promise to be my wife?'

"'I promise.'"

"'And your promise shall be irrevocable?'"

"She turned on him with scorn. 'The promise of a lady is ever irrevocable,' she said.

"'Ah!' cried Voltaire, 'love is a stronger passion than vengeance, and my love will win yours.'"

"'Meanwhile,' she went on without noticing this rhapsody, 'if you breathe one word or utter one sound by which suspicion can fall on Mr. Blake, my promise is forfeited; if you stay here after to-morrow, or attempt to see me within this and next Christmas Eve, my promise is also forfeited.'"

"'What, am I to leave you at once?'"

"'At once.'"

"He left the room immediately after," said Tom, "while, after saying 'Good-night' to me, she too retired to her bedroom."

To say that I was astonished at the turn things had taken would not give the slightest idea of my feelings. And yet a great joy filled my heart. The sword of Damocles, which seemed to hang over my head, possessed no terror.

"Is that all, Tom?" I said at length.

"This morning, as I told you, he arranged for Kaffar's luggage to be sent to Egypt, while he himself is preparing to depart."

"Where is he going?"

"To London."

"And Miss Forrest?"

"She, I hope, will stay with us for some time. But, Justin, can you really give no explanation of these things? Surely you must be able to?"

"I cannot, Tom. I am hedged in on every side. I'm enslaved, and I cannot tell you how. My life is a mystery, and at times a terror."

"But do you know what has become of Kaffar?"

"No more than that dog barking in the yard. All is dark to me."

Tom left me then, while I, with my poor tired brain, tried to think what to do.

Joseph Hocking

CHAPTER XIII

A MESMERIST'S SPELL

I found on entering the breakfast-room that my presence caused no surprise, neither did any of the guests regard me suspiciously. It had gone abroad that I had gone out to find Kaffar, but was unable to do so; and as Voltaire had publicly spoken of Kaffar's luggage being sent to Cairo, there was, to them, no mystery regarding him.

Several spoke of his going away as being a good riddance, and declared him to be unfit for respectable society; but I did not answer them, and after a while the subject dropped.

Voltaire, however, was not in the room; and when, after having breakfasted, I was wondering where he was, I felt the old terrible sensation come over me. I tried to resist the influence that was drawing me out of the room, but I could not. I put on my overcoat and hat, and, drawn on by an unseen power, I went away towards the fir plantation in which the summer-house was built.

As I knew I should, I found Voltaire there. He smiled on me and lifted his hat politely. "I thought I would allow you to have a good breakfast before summoning you," he said, "especially as this is the last conversation we shall have for some time."

I thought I detected a look of triumph in his eyes, yet I was sure he regarded me with intense hatred.

"Yes," I said, "I am come. What is your will now?"

"This. I find that Mr. Temple has told you about an interview which was held in the library last night."

"Yes; it is true."

"Do you know of what you are in danger?"

"No—what?"

"Hanging."

"What for?"

"For murdering Kaffar."

"Did I kill him? I remember nothing. What was done was not because of me, but because of the demon that caused me blindly to act."

"Names are cheap, my man, and I don't mind. Claptrap morality is nothing to me. Yes, you killed Kaffar—killed him with that knife you held in your hand. I meant that you should. Kaffar was getting troublesome to me, and I wanted to get him out of the way. To use you as I did was killing two birds with one stone. You know that Miss Forrest has promised to marry me if Kaffar be not forthcoming by next Christmas Eve. That, of course, can never be, so my beautiful bride is safe;" and he looked at me with a savage leer.

"Have you brought me here to tell me that?"

"No; but to tell you a little good news. I have decided to hold you as the slave to my will until the day Miss Gertrude Forrest becomes Mrs. Herod Voltaire, and then to set you free. Meanwhile, I want to give you a few instructions."

"What are they?"

"You are not to take one step in trying to prove that Kaffar is alive."

"Ah!" I cried; "you fear I might produce him. Then I have not killed him, even through you. Thank God! thank God!"

"Stop your pious exclamations," he said. "No, you are wrong. You did kill Kaffar, and he lies at the bottom of yonder ghostly pool; so that is not the reason. Why I do not wish you to search for him is that thereby you might find out things about me that I do not wish you to do. In such a life as mine there are naturally things that I do not wish known. In going to my old haunts, trying to unearth Kaffar, you would learn something about them. And so I command you," he continued, in a hoarse tone that made me shudder, "that you do not move one step in that direction. If you do—well, you know my power."

From that moment I felt more enslaved than ever. I shuddered at the thought of disobeying him; I felt more than ever a lost man. As I felt at that moment, in spite of my desire to let every one know this man's power over me, I would rather have pulled out my tongue than have done so.

"Are those all your commands?" I said humbly.

"Ah! you are cowed at last, are you?" he said mockingly.

"You matched your strength with mine; now you know what it means. You did not think I could crush you like a grasshopper, did you? Yes, I have one other command for you. You must go to London to-morrow, and go on with your old work. You must not hold any communication with Miss Forrest, my affianced bride. I myself am going to London to-day, and most likely shall remain there for a while. Perhaps I shall want to see you occasionally. If I do, you will quickly know. I shall have no need to tell you my address;" and he laughed a savage laugh.

"Is that all?" I said.

"That is all. You will come to the wedding, Mr. Blake. You shall see her arrayed for her husband, dressed all in white, as a bride should be. You shall see her lips touch mine. You shall see us go away together—the woman you love, and the man who has crushed you as if you were a worm."

This maddened me. By a tremendous effort of will I was free. "That shall never be. Somehow, some way, I will thwart you," I cried. "I will free myself from you; I will snap your cruel chain asunder."

"I defy you!" he said. "You can do nothing that I have commanded you not to do. For the rest I care not a jot."

He went away, leaving me alone, and then all the sensations of the previous nights came back to me. I remembered what the ghost was supposed to foretell, and the evil influence the dark pond was said to have. I saw again the large red hand on the water's surface. I recalled dimly the struggle, the fighting, the strange feeling I had as my senses began to leave me. Could I have killed him? If I did, I was guiltless of crime. It was not my heart that conceived the thought; it was not I who really did the deed. I had no pangs of conscience, no feeling of remorse, and yet the thought that I had hurried a man into eternity was horrible.

I wandered in the plantation for hours, brooding, thinking, despairing. No pen can describe what I felt, no words can convey to the mind the thoughts and pains of my mind and heart. Never did I love Miss Forrest so much, never was Voltaire's villainy so real; and yet I was to lose her, and that man—a fiend in human form—was to wed her. I could do nothing. He had paralyzed my energies. He had set a command before me which was as ghastly as hell, and yet I dared not disobey. I, a young, strong man, was a slave—a slave of the worst kind. I was the plaything, the tool of a villain. I had to do as he told me; I had to refrain from doing what he told me I was not to do. I had done I knew not what. Perchance a hangman's rope was hanging near me even now. I could not tell. And yet I dared not rise from my chains, and see whether the things I had been accused of doing were true.

I went back to the house. Voltaire was gone, while the guests and family were having their lunch. I felt that I could not join them, so I went into the library. I had not been there ten minutes when Miss Forrest entered. She looked pale and worried. I suppose that I, too, must have been haggard, for she started when she saw me. She hesitated a moment, and then spoke.

"The whole party are going for a ride this afternoon. They have just been making arrangements. They are going to ask you to join them. Shall you go?" she asked.

"No; I shall not go," I replied.

"Will you come here at three o'clock?"

"Yes," I said, wondering what she meant; but I had not time to ask her, for two young men came into the room.

I went to my room and tried to think, but I could not. My mind refused to work. I watched the party ride away—it was comparatively small now, for several had returned to their homes—and then I found my way to the library.

I sat for a while in silence, scarcely conscious of my surroundings; and then I wondered how long Miss Forrest would be before she came, and what she would tell me. The clock on the mantelpiece began to strike three; it had not finished when she entered the room.

I placed a chair for her beside my own, which she accepted without a word.

For a minute neither of us spoke; then she said abruptly, "You told me you loved me when we rode out together the other day."

"I did," I said, "and I do love you with all the intensity that a human heart is capable of loving; but it is hopeless now."

"Why?"

"You have promised to marry another man."

"What do you know of this?"

Both of us were very excited. We were moved to talk in an unconventional strain.

"Mr. Temple told me of your interview together last night."

A slight flush came to her face. "But Mr. Temple has told

you the condition of the promise as well," she said.

"Yes; but that condition makes me hopeless."

"What!" she cried. "But no, I will not entertain such a thought. You are as innocent as I am."

"Yes, I am innocent in thought, in intent, and in heart; but as for the deed itself, I know not."

"I do not understand you," she said; "you speak in words that convey no meaning to my mind. Will you explain?"

"I cannot, Miss Forrest. I would give all I possess if I could. I have nothing that I would keep secret from you, and yet I cannot tell you that which you would know."

Did she understand me? Did her quick mind guess my condition? I could not tell, and yet a strange look of intelligence flashed from her eyes.

"Mr. Blake," she said, "my soul loathes the thought of marrying that man. If ever my promise has to be fulfilled, I shall die the very day on which he calls me wife."

My heart gave a great throb of joy; her every word gave me hope in spite of myself.

"Mr. Blake," she continued, "I never must marry him."

"God grant you may not," I said.

"I must not," she said, "and you must keep me from danger."

"I, Miss Forrest! I would give the world if I could: but how can I? You do not know the terrible slavery that binds me, neither can I tell you."

"I shall trust in you to deliver me from this man," she went on without heeding me. "You must prove yourself to be innocent."

"To do that I must bring this man Kaffar. I know nothing of him. I could never find him. Oh, I tell you, Miss Forrest, a thousand evil powers seem to rend me when I attempt to do what I long for."

"I shall trust in you," she cried. "Surely you are sufficiently interested in me to save me from a man like Voltaire?"

"Interested?" I cried. "I would die for you, I love you so. And yet I can do nothing."

"You can do something; you can do everything. You can save me from him."

"Oh," I cried, "I know I must appear a pitiful coward to you. It is for me you have placed yourself in this position, while I refuse to try to liberate you from it. If I only could; if I dared! But I am chained on every hand."

"But you are going to break those chains; you are going to be free; you are going to be happy."

Her words nerved me. The impossible seemed possible, and yet everything was misty.

"Only one thing can make me happy," I said, "and that can never be now. I have lost my strength; I am become a pitiful coward."

"You are going to be happy!" she repeated.

"Miss Forrest," I said, "do not mock me. My life for days has been a hell. I have had a terrible existence; no light shines in the sky. You cannot think what your words mean to me, or you would not speak them."

"Will you not, for my sake, if not for your own, exert yourself? Will you not think of my happiness a little? The thought of marrying that man is madness."

"Miss Forrest," I cried, "you must think I have lost all manhood, all self-respect, when you hear what I say; but the only thing that could make me think of trying to do what is ten thousand times my duty to do, is that you will give me some hope that, if I should succeed, you will be the wife of such a poor thing as I am."

She looked at me intently. She was very pale, and her eyes shone like stars. Beautiful she looked beyond compare, and so grand, so noble. She was tied down to no conventionalities; whither her pure true heart led her, she followed.

"If you succeed," she said, "I will be your wife."

"But not simply from a feeling of pity?" I cried. "I could not let you do that. I have manliness enough for that even yet."

"No," she said proudly, "but because you are the only man I ever did or can love."

For a minute I forgot my woes, my pains. No ghastly deed taunted me with its memory, no dark cloud hung in the skies. I felt my Gertrude's lips against mine; I felt that her life was given to me. I was no longer alone and desolate; a pure, beautiful woman had trusted me so fully, so truly, that hope dawned in my sky, and earth was heaven.

"Now, Justin," she said, after a few minutes of happy silence, "you must away. Every hour may be precious. God knows how gladly I would be with you, but it must not be. But remember, my hope lies in you, and my love is given to you. God bless you!"

She went away then and left me; while I, without knowing why, prepared to start for London.

I had a great work to do. I had, if I was to win Gertrude for my wife, to break and crush Voltaire's power over me. I had to find Kaffar, if he was to be found, and that to me was an awful uncertainty, and I had to bring him to Gertrude before the next Christmas Eve.

Away from her the skies were dark again, great heavy weights rested on my heart, and my life seemed clogged. Still her love had nerved me to do what I otherwise could never have done. It had nerved me to try; and so, with her warm kiss burning on my lips, I hurried off to the great metropolis without any definite idea why I was going.

Joseph Hocking

CHAPTER XIV

GOD

For the next three months I was an atheist! These are easy words to write, but terrible to realize. No one but those who know can tell the terror of a man who has given up belief in an Eternal Goodness, in a living God that cares for man.

I left Yorkshire with some little hope in my heart—the memory of Gertrude's words was with me, cheering me during the long ride; but when once alone in my rooms, nothing but a feeling of utter desolation possessed my heart. The terrible night on the Yorkshire moors came back again, the dark forbidding waters, the ghastly red hand, the gleaming knife, the struggle—all were real. Did I kill him? I did not know. Possibly I was a murderer in act, if not in thought. I could not bear to think of it. Who can bear to think of having taken away a fellow-creature's life? And he might be lying in Drearwater Pond even then!

Then there was the terrible spell that this man had cast upon me. I felt it clinging to every fibre of my being. I was not living a true life; I was living a dual life. A power extraneous to myself, and yet possessing me, made me a mere machine. As the days and weeks passed away things became worse. I promised Gertrude to exert myself to find Kaffar, to set her free from her promise to Voltaire; but I could not do it. His command was upon me. I felt that it was ever in his mind that I should not make any efforts, and I had to obey. And his power was evil, his motives were fiendish, his nature was depraved. Still preachers talked of a loving God, of the good being stronger than the evil. It could not be.

"Try! Try! Resist! Resist! Struggle! Struggle!" said hope and duty and love; and I tried, I resisted, I struggled. And still I was bound in chains; still I was held by a mysterious occult power.

Then it ceased to feel to be a duty to rid Gertrude of Voltaire. Why should I struggle and resist? Supposing I succeeded, was I any more fit to be her husband than he? What was I? At best a poor weak creature, the plaything of a villain. At any time he could exert his power and make me his slave. But I might be worse than that. I might, with my own hand, have sent a man into eternity. How did I know it was Voltaire's power that made me do the deed? Might not my blind passion have swept me on to this dark deed? But that could not be. No, no; I could not believe that. Besides, Voltaire had told me it was because of him. Still, I was not fit to be her husband.

Then her words came back to me, and her pure influence gave me strength. She, so pure, so true, had seemed to understand my position, had bid me hope and be brave. She had told me she loved me—she, whom hundreds of brave men would love to call their own. I would try again. I *would* brake the chains Voltaire had forged; I WOULD hurl from me the incubus that would otherwise crush me.

I tried again, and again; and again, and again I failed.

I did not pray. I could not. If God cared, I thought, He would help the innocent. I was innocent in thought, and still I was not helped. God did not care, for He helped me not. Months had passed away, and I had taken no forward step. I was still enslaved. The preachers were wrong; God did not care for the beings He had made.

There was no God.

God meant "the good one." "God is eternally good, all-powerful, if there is a God. But there is not," I said. Evil was rampant. Every day vice triumphed, every day virtue suffered. Goodness was not the strongest force. Vice was conquering; evil powers were triumphant. Why should any exception be made for me? If there is a God, evil would be checked, destroyed; instead of which, it was conquering every day. There could be no God; and if no God, good and evil were little more than names. We were the sport of chance, and chance meant the destruction of anything like moral responsibility. I could not help being constituted as I was, neither could Voltaire help his nature. One set of circumstances had surrounded his life, another mine, and our image and shape were according to the force of these circumstances. As for a God who loved us, it was absurd.

And yet who gave us love—made us capable of loving? Was love the result of chance, which was in reality nothing? And again, whence the idea of God, whence the longing for Him? Besides, did not the longing for Him give evidence of His being?

But I will not weary the reader with my mental wanderings; they are doubtless wearisome enough, and yet they were terribly real to me Although I have used but a few pages of paper in hinting at them, they caused me to lie awake through many a weary night.

Still no help came.

I went to a church one Sunday night. There was nothing of importance that struck me during the service, save the reading of one of the lessons. It was the story of the youth who was possessed with a devil, which the disciples could not cast out. The minister was, I should think, a good man, for he read it naturally, and with a great deal of power; and when he came to the part where Jesus came and caused the evil spirit to come out of him, my heart throbbed with joy. Was there hope for me? Was Jesus Christ still the same wonderful power? Was He here now—to help, to save?

That was at the end of three months.

I went home and prayed—prayed to be delivered from the evil power which chained me.

I might as well have turned my thoughts in another direction for all the good I could see it did me. The old numbing feeling still possessed me. My little spark of faith began to die. It was foolishness to think of God, I said.

A week later, I walked in Hyde Park. An evil influence seemed to draw me in the direction of the Marble Arch. I had not gone far, when I met Voltaire. I knew then that I was more in his power than ever. He did not speak—he only looked; but it was a look of victory, of power.

I got into Oxford Street and got on a 'bus. Mechanically I bought a paper, one of the leading dailies. Listlessly I opened it, and the first words that caught my eyes were "Reviews of Books." I glanced down the column, and saw the words, "David Elginbrod," by George Macdonald. "This book is one of remarkable power," the paper went on to say, "and will appeal to the highest class of minds. Its interest is more than ordinary, because it deals with the fascinating subjects of Animal Magnetism, Mesmerism, and Spiritualism. Moreover, Dr. Macdonald shows what enormous power, for evil or for good, may be exerted by it; indeed, the principal characters in the story are so influenced by it, that the author is led to make quite a study of these occult sciences."

I did not read the review further; what I had read was sufficient to determine me to buy the book. Accordingly, on my arrival in the City, I obtained a copy; and then, with all possible haste, I made my way home, and, throwing myself in a chair, sat down to read it.

I did not cease reading until I had finished what I regarded then, and still regard, as one of the finest religious novels of the age. This may seem to many extravagant praise; but when I remember the influence it had on my life, I feel inclined to hold to my opinion.

Putting aside the other parts of the book, that in which I was so fearfully interested might be briefly stated thus:—

Mesmerism and animal magnetism may be regarded as human forces. Those possessing them, and thereby having the power to mesmerize, may subjugate the will of those who are susceptible to mesmeric influences, and hold them in a complete and terrible slavery. The oftener the victim yields to the will of the mesmerist, the stronger will his power become. There is only one means by which the person under this influence can be free. This is by obtaining a strength superior to that of the mesmerist, which is only to be realized by being in communion with a Higher Life, and participating in that Life. Only the Divine power in the life of the victim can make him possess a power superior to the mesmerist's. Possessing that, he becomes free, because he possesses a life superior to mere physical or human power.

The victim in the book is led to seek that Divine Life in her, and although she loses her physical life, she dies freed from the terrible thraldom which has been cursing her existence.

That is all I need write concerning the book I have mentioned, i.e. descriptive of its teaching.

It turned my mind into a new channel. The teaching seemed scientific and reasonable. If there were a God, who was the Source of all life, He could, by entering into the life of any individual, give him such forces as would be superior to any other force. This was true, further, because all evil was in opposition to the laws of the universe, and thus the good must overcome the evil.

This, however, I clearly saw: if I would possess the power of God in me, I must submit myself wholly and unreservedly to Him. He had made me a free agent, and I must allow Him to possess me wholly.

I will not describe what followed. It is too sacred a subject to parade. We cannot write on paper our deepest feelings; we cannot describe in words the yearnings and experiences of the soul. Were I to try I could give no adequate idea of my hopes and fears, my prayers and struggles. To realize my life, a similar condition must be experienced.

I ask, however, that I may be believed when I say this: a month later I really believed in God, and soon I began to realize His power. I felt a new life growing in me, a higher life. I began to be possessed of a power whereby I could conquer myself, subjugate my own will, and be master over my passions. The reader may smile as he or she reads this, but this is true: when I became possessed of a life whereby I became master of my lower self, I felt free from Voltaire's power. I realized that to be master over myself meant being a slave to none.

I was free, and I knew it. A fuller, richer life surged within me, enabling me to rise above the occult forces of our physical and mental natures. Hope lived within me, and confidence as to the future began to inspire me.

CHAPTER XV

BEGINNING TO SEARCH

No sooner did I begin to feel freed from Voltaire's power than I began to exert myself to find Kaffar, if indeed he were to be found. There was much in my favour. I possessed freedom; I had plenty of money; I had plenty of time. On the other hand, there was much against me. Was he alive? Were Voltaire's words true? Had I in my mesmeric condition yielded to his will in such a degree as to kill the wily Egyptian and hurl him in the pond? Again, if he were alive, where was he? Who could tell? Supposing he had gone to Egypt, how could I find him? Possibly he had a thousand haunts unknown to me.

I determined to go to Yorkshire, and soon found myself within the hospitable walls of Temple Hall. The house was very quiet, however for which I was very glad. I wanted to talk quietly with Tom; I wanted to investigate the whole matter.

When I had finished telling Tom my story, he seemed perfectly astounded.

"What, Justin!" he exclaimed, "do you mean to say that the villain used such means to get you out of his road and win

Miss Forrest for himself?"

"I felt he was unscrupulous when I first met him," I replied. "I am sure he guessed my secret, and determined to get me out of the way by fair means or by foul."

We talked long concerning the matter; we tried to recall all that had been said and done; but, in spite of all, we could not hit upon any plan of action.

"Do you think she will marry Voltaire," I said, after a short silence, "if I cannot find Kaffar or prove that he is alive?"

"I am sure she will, Justin. Never did I meet with any one who has a higher sense of honour than she. I believe she would rather die than do a mean thing."

"And yet," I said wearily, "I am almost certain I did not kill Kaffar. I can remember nothing distinctly, and yet I have the consciousness that I never struck him a blow."

"And I, too, am sure you did not do this, Justin," replied Tom. "I felt that he was acting, in spite of the terrible evidence against you. But what is the use? If you cannot find the Egyptian, he will marry Miss Forrest, and after that— well, all seems hopeless."

"It shall not be hopeless," I said. "If he is alive, he shall be found, and I will bring him back, and she shall see him."

"Ah, yes; and that reminds me, Justin, she bade me tell you that she would be in her own home at Kensington until after the next new year."

This made me joyful in spite of everything. She still had an interest in me; she still believed me innocent.

"By the way, Tom," I said, after another short silence, "have you found out anything in relation to the ghost which appeared here during my visit?"

"Nothing definite. Stay, I forgot. Simon Slowden said he had something particular to tell you when you came to Yorkshire again. I asked him the subject of this 'something particular,' and he said it was about the ghost. I tried to make him explain further, but could not."

"I'll see Simon at once," I said. "I cannot afford to let anything pass without examining it. Any little thing might give a clue to the mystery."

I sought Simon in the stable-yard, and found him as grim and platonic as ever.

"Glad to see yer honour," said Simon, hastily. "I've made up my mind scores of times to write a letter, but I hev had sich bad luck wi' letters, that I 'adn't the necessary quantity o' pluck, you know."

"Bad luck with your letters, Simon? How?"

"Why, yer see, yer honour, after the doctor experimented on me by waccinatin' me agin' small-pox, cholera, and the measles, together wi' 'oopin' cough and several other baby complaints as 'ev a hinjurious effect upon people as 'ev cut their wisdom teeth, you know as I told yer honour that I caught that 'ere werry disease of small-pox which spiled my beauty for ever. Well, as I told yer months ago, I went to the 'ousemaid for a mite 'o comfort, and catches 'er a-courtin' wi' the coachman. So I goes 'ome, and I says I'll write 'er a letter as would charm a dead duck in a saucepan. So I begins my letter this yer way: 'My dearest dear,' I says, 'times es bad, and people be glad to catch anything; so I, thinkin' small-pox better than nothin', catched that. Forgive me, and I'll never do so no more. I'm cryin' all the day, as though I got my livin' wi' skinnin' onions. Relieve me, my dear, or my feelin's will be too much for me. They be fillin' me faster 'n I can dispose of 'em; and if you don't leave that 'ere coachman and smile on me, I shall either go up like a baloon, or else there'll be a case of combustion.' I went on in that 'ere style, yer know, thinkin' she'd melt like a h'yster in a fryin'-pan, but she didn't; and the next thing I hears wus that the coachman wur at the willage alehouse readin' my letter. Since then I've guv up the tender passion and guv up writin' letters."

"Well, you have had bad luck, Simon; but perhaps you'll be more fortunate next time. Mr. Temple tells me you have something to tell me about the ghost. What is it?"

"You ain't a-seen that 'ere hinfidel willain since he went away from 'ere, Mr. Blake, have 'ee?"

"I saw him in Hyde Park one day, but have never spoken to him."

"Well, I'm in a fog."

"In a fog! How?"

"Why, I can't understand a bit why that 'ere ghost wur a got up."

"You think it was got up, then?"

"Certain of it, yer honour."

"Well, tell us about it."

"Well, sur, after you left all of a hurry like, we had a big party in the house, and all the servants 'ad to 'elp; and no sooner did I git in that 'ere house than I beginned to put two and two together, and then I see a hindiwidual that I beginned to think wur mighty like that 'ere ghost."

"And who was that?"

"Why, that 'ere hancient wirgin, Miss Staggles."

"Ah, what then?"

"Well, I heard somebody tellin' her as 'ow you were gone to London, and I thought she looked mighty pleased. After dinner, I see her come out of the drawin'-room, and go away by herself, and I thought I'd watch. She went up to her room, yer honour, and I got in a convenient place for watchin' her when she comes out. She weren't a minnit afore she wur out, Mr. Blake, a-carryin' somethin' in her hands. She looks curiously 'round, and then I see her make straight for your bedroom door, and goes into your room. In a minnit more she comes out, with nothin' in her hands. So then I says to myself, 'She's deposited some o' her combustible matter in Mr. Blake's room.'"

"It was a bold and dangerous thing to do, yer honour, but I goes into your room and looks around. Everything seems right. Then I looks and sees that the drawer of the wardrobe ain't quite shut, so I takes a step forward and peeps in."

"And what did you see?"

"Why, I see the trappin's of that 'ere ghost. The shroud, knife, and all the rest on't."

"Well, Simon?"

Joseph Hocking

"Well, sur, I takes it to my shanty, and puts it in my own box, to show you at 'a convenient season,' as Moses said."

"Is that all?"

"Not quite. The next mornin' I see her a-airin' her sweet self on the lawn, so I goes up to 'er all familiar like, and I says, 'Top o' the mornin', Miss Staggles.'"

"'Who are you, man?' she says."

"'As nice a chap as you ever see,' I said, 'though I am marked wi' small-pox. But that ain't my fault, ma'am; it is owin' to the experimentin' o' a waccinatin' doctor.'"

"'What do you want with me, man?' she said."

"'Why, ma'am,' I said, 'I'm young and simple, and I wur frightened wi' a ghost t'other night, and I thought as how you, bein' purty hancient, might assist me in findin' things out about it.'"

"With that, sur, she looked oal strange, and I thinks I'm on the right track, and I says again, 'That 'ere ghost wur well got up, mum. I've played a ghost myself in a theatre, and I could never git up like you did the other night.'"

"'Me get up as a ghost!' she screamed. 'Man, you are mad.'"

"'Not so mad,' I says, 'seein' as 'ow I see you carry that 'ere ghost's wardrobe, and put it in Mr. Blake's room last night.'"

"She went off without another word, yer honour, and the next thing I heard 'bout her was that she'd gone to London."

"And why did you not tell Mr. Temple?"

"Well, Mr. Blake, he didn't know anything 'bout her evenin' rambles wi' that 'ere hinfidel willain, and wasn't acquainted wi' the things that you and me hev talked about; besides, I thought as 'ow you wer the one that ought to know first of all."

I thought long over Simon's words, but could not understand them. Why should Miss Staggles pose as a ghost, even at the instigation of Voltaire? There could be nothing gained by it, and yet I was sure that it was not without meaning. Somehow it was connected with Voltaire's scheme; of that I was sure, but at the time my mind was too confused to see how.

So far, not one step had been taken to prove whether Kaffar was dead or alive, and although I knew nothing of a detective's business, I did not like taking any one into my confidence. I resolved to do all that was to be done myself.

In spite of everything, I spent a pleasant evening at Temple Hall. We talked and laughed gaily, especially as Tom was preparing for his wedding with Miss Edith Gray, and when I told Mrs. Temple how Tom had popped the question on the landing at midnight, after the appearance of the famous hall ghost, the merriment knew no bounds.

It was after midnight when I retired to rest, but I could not sleep. I could not help thinking about this great problem of my life. How could I find Kaffar? How could I tell whether he were alive or dead? After tossing about a long time, I hit upon a plan of action, and then my mind had some little rest.

The next morning I bade good-bye to my friends, and started for the station. When I arrived all was quiet. Not a single passenger was there, while the two porters were lolling lazily around, enjoying the warmth of the bright May sun.

Joseph Hocking

I asked to see the station-master; he was not at the station. Then I made inquiries for the booking-clerk, who presently made his appearance. I found that there was a train leaving about midnight, which travelled northward, one that had been running some years.

"Were you at the booking-office on the day after New Year's Day?" I asked.

"Yes, sir," replied the clerk.

"Do you remember a man coming for a ticket that night who struck you as peculiar?"

"What kind of a man, sir?"

"A foreigner. Small, dark, and wiry, speaking with an accent something like this," I said, trying to imitate Kaffar.

"No, sir, I don't remember such a person. There were only three passengers that night—I remember it very well, because my brother was here with me—and they were all Yorkshire."

"This midnight train is a stopping train?"

"Yes, sir. It stops at every station from Leeds."

"How far is the nearest station in the Leeds direction?"

"Seven miles, sir. The population is rather thin here, sir. It gets thicker the closer you get to Leeds."

"And how far the other way?"

"Only a matter of three miles northward, sir. There's a little village there, sir, has sprung up because of Lord—'s mansion, sir, and the company has put up a station."

"And how far is the next station beyond that?"

"A long way, sir. It's a junction where some go to catch the night express to Leeds. It must be eight miles further on. The train is now due, sir, that goes there."

"And it stops at the next station?"

"Oh yes, sir."

I booked immediately for it, and in a few minutes arrived there. It was, if possible, more quiet than the one from which I had just come; a more dreary place one could not well see.

I soon found the man who had issued tickets on the night I have mentioned. Did he remember such a passenger as I described?

"Yes, sir," he said, "I do remember such a chap; partly because he was the only passenger, and partly because he looked so strange. He looked as if he'd been fightin', and yet he was quite sober. He was a funny chap, sir; one as I shudd'n like much to do wi'."

"And where did he book for?"

"Dingledale Junction, sir."

"And he would be able to catch a train from there?"

"He would have to wait a quarter of an hour for the express to Leeds," replied the man.

"And how long will it be before there's another train to Dingledale Junction?" I asked anxiously.

"Three hours and a half, sir."

This was an awful blow to me. To wait all this time at that roadside station was weary work, especially as I could do nothing. I found, however, that I could hire a horse and trap that would take me there in about two hours. I therefore closed with this offer, and shortly after drove away.

I felt sure I had made one step forward. Kaffar was alive. The blunt Yorkshireman's description of him tallied exactly with the real appearance of the Egyptian. Of course I was not sure, but this was strongly in favour of his being alive. There was something tangible for which to work now, and my heart grew lighter.

Dingledale Junction proved to be rather a busy place. There were two platforms in the station, and a refreshment room. I found also that Mr. Smith was actually represented there, in the shape of a small boy, a dozen novels, and a few newspapers. This, however, did not augur so well for my inquiries. The officials here would not be so likely to notice any particular passenger. Still there was something in my favour. Kaffar would in any circumstances attract attention in a country place. His appearance was so remarkable, that any countryman would stop for a second look at him.

After a great many inquiries, I found that Kaffar, or a man strongly resembling him, had been there on the night in question, and had taken a ticket for Leeds. He had no luggage, and what made the porter in attendance remember him so vividly was the fact of his being angry when asked if he had any luggage to be labelled.

So far, then, my inquiries were successful; so far I might congratulate myself on making forward steps. And yet I was scarcely satisfied. It seemed too plain. Would Kaffar have allowed himself to be followed in such a way? I was not sure. On the one hand, he was very cunning, and, on the other, he knew but little of the means of detecting people in England.

I took the next train for Leeds, and there my success ended. I could find traces of him nowhere. This was scarcely to be wondered at. Leeds is a great commercial centre, where men of every nationality meet, and of course Kaffar would be allowed to pass unnoticed. Then I began to think what the Egyptian would be likely to do, and after weighing the whole matter in my mind I came to this conclusion: either he was in London with Voltaire, or he had gone back to Egypt. The first was not likely. If Kaffar were seen in London, Voltaire's plans would be upset, and I did not think my enemy would allow that. Of course he might have means of keeping him there in strict secrecy, or he might have a score of disguises to keep him from detection. Still I thought the balance would be heaviest on the side of his returning to Egypt. I naturally thought he would return to his native land, because I had heard him say he talked none of the European languages besides English and a smattering of Turkish.

My next step, therefore, was to return to London, and then go to Dover, Calais, Newhaven, and Dieppe, to try to see whether Kaffar could be traced. At the same time, I determined to have a watch set upon Voltaire, and his every step dogged, so that, if he held any communication with Kaffar, necessary steps might be taken to prove to Miss Forrest my innocence, and thus she might at once be freed from the designs of the man she hated.

No sooner did I arrive in London, however, and took

possession of my easy-chair than I knew Voltaire wanted me to go to him, and I knew, too, that a month before I should have had to yield to the power he possessed. I need not say that I did not go. My will was now stronger than his, and by exercising that will I was able to resist him. Still, none but those who have been under such a spell can imagine what a struggle I had even then. God only gives us power to use, and He will not do for us what we can do for ourselves. For two long hours I felt this strange influence, and then it ceased. Evidently he had failed in his design, and, for the time, at all events, had abandoned it.

Next morning, when I was preparing to visit Scotland Yard, a servant came into my room bearing a card on a tray. I took it and read, "Herod Voltaire."

"Show him up," I said to the servant.

CHAPTER XVI

STRUGGLING FOR VICTORY

I confess that I was somewhat excited as I heard him coming up the stairs. I was sure that every means he could devise to defeat me would be eagerly used. The man was a villain possessed of a strange and dangerous power, and that power he would not hesitate to exert in every possible way. But I was not afraid; my faith in God had given me life, and so I would dare to defy the wretch.

I did not look at him until the girl had shown him in and left the room; then our eyes met.

I recognized the steely glitter of those whity-grey orbs, which at times seemed tinted with green. I knew he was seeking to exert his old influence, and once I thought I should have to yield. The power he possessed was something terrible, and I had to struggle to the utmost to remain unconquered. His efforts were in vain, however, and, for the time, at all events, the battle was not with him.

"Will you sit down, Mr. Voltaire?" I said, after a minute's perfect silence.

He sat down as if in astonishment.

"Might I ask your business?" I asked as coolly as I could.

This question either aroused his anger, or he began to play a part. "Yes," he said; "you will know my business at your cost. I thought you had found out before this that I was not the man either to be disobeyed or trifled with."

I did not think it wise to speak.

"I have come to tell you," he went on, "that you cannot escape my power, that you cannot disobey me and not suffer. Remember this: I conquered you, and you are my slave."

Still I did not think it wise to reply.

"You think," he continued, "because you have realized some immunity from the power I wield, that I have left you. I have not, and it is greater than ever. You have dared to leave London; you have dared to do that which I told you not; and now I have come to tell you that you have aroused the anger of a man who laughs at conventional laws, and snaps his fingers at the ordinary usages of society—one who knows nothing and cares nothing for your claptrap morality, and will not be influenced by it."

"I am sorry if I have angered you," I replied humbly.

"Just so, and you will be more than sorry. Man, I hold your life in the hollow of my hand. One word from me, and your liberty is gone; you will be dragged through the streets like a common felon."

"Am I guilty of so much, then?" I said. "Did I really kill that man?"

He looked at me curiously, as if he suspected something.

"Kill him?" he replied. "Of course you did. But even if you did not, it is all the same. Kaffar cannot be found, or proved alive, and thus my power over you is absolute."

"I wonder you do not use it," I said quietly.

"I do not use it because it does not pay me to do so. My policy is to be quiet. Miss Forrest is mine because she knows I am master of your life. The months are swiftly passing away, Mr. Justin Blake. It is May now; in December I shall take her to my breast."

"But supposing," I said, "that I find Kaffar; supposing before Christmas Eve comes I prove I am innocent of his death. What then?"

"It is not to be supposed. You killed my friend; and even if you did not, you could never find him. You dare not, could not, take any necessary steps. You have not the power to ask other people to do it. Even now you cannot rise from your seat and walk across the room."

Without a word I rose from my seat and walked across the room; then I came back and coolly sat down again.

"What does this mean?" he asked angrily.

"It means," I said, "that you are deceived—mistaken. It means that your villainous schemes are of no effect; that the man whom you thought you had entrapped by a juggler's trick to be your tool and dupe is as free as you are; that he defies your power; that he tells you to do your worst."

I felt that again he was trying to throw me into a kind of trance, that he was exerting all his power and knowledge; but I resisted, and I was free. I stood up again and smiled.

Then a strange light lit up his eyes.

"Curse you!" he cried, "you defy me, eh? Well, you'll see what you get by defying me. In five minutes you will be safe in a policeman's charge."

"If I were you I would try and learn the Englishman's laws before you appeal to them. The first question that will be asked will be why you have refrained from telling so long, for he who shelters a criminal by silence is regarded as an aider and an abettor of that criminal. Then, man, this case will be sifted to the bottom. That pond will be pumped dry, and every outlet examined. Besides, what about the booking-clerk that issued a ticket to Kaffar two hours after you and Mr. Temple found me?"

"It's a lie!" he cried; "Kaffar was never seen."

"Well, then, if you are so sure, give me in charge. It will not be very much opposed to my wishes, for by so doing you will set the whole machinery of the law of England on Kaffar's trail, and I promise you it will find him. English law is hard on murderers, but all evidence is put through a very fine sieve in an English court of justice. Kaffar is not an ordinary-looking man, and from Scotland Yard our police authorities hold communication with all other police authorities in the civilized world. I tell you, man, your trumped-up story would be torn to pieces in five minutes, and in the end you would be safely lodged down at Dartmoor for fourteen years."

He sat silent a minute, as if in deep thought; then he said slowly, "Mr. Justin Blake, you think you have outwitted Herod Voltaire! Continue to think so. I shall not give you in charge—not because I believe in your paltry story, but because I should lose Miss Forrest by so doing, and I cannot afford to do that, if for nothing else than to spite you. You think you are free from me. Wait. You think Kaffar is to be found—well, wait. But, I tell you, you shall repent all this. I will marry the woman you love, and then I will lead you such a life as you never conceived. You shall pray to die, and death shall not come. You shall suffer as never man suffered. The condition of the Christians whom Nero used as torches shall be heaven to what yours shall be. Meanwhile—"

All this time he kept looking at me, and his words were uttered with a nervous force and intensity that was terrible. I felt a strange chilling sensation creep over me, and involuntarily I sat down. No sooner had I done so than he gave a savage, exultant yell.

"You are mine again!" he cried.

It was a terrible struggle. His will and mine fought for the mastery—his strengthened by a knowledge of laws of which I was ignorant, and constant exertion of it; mine, by a new life which I had but lately begun to live, by a strength given me through communion with my Maker.

For a minute I was chained to the seat. My senses were numbed, and, all the while his terrible glittering eyes rested on mine. Then my strength began to return, and I again stood up, and in a few seconds I was master of myself.

"Coward," I said, "you sought to take me unawares. You have done your utmost, and I am your master, even now. Now go, and bear this in mind, that the right and the truth shall be triumphant."

I rung the bell as I spoke, and the servant appeared. "Show this gentleman out, Mary," I said.

Never shall I forget the look of hatred that gleamed from his eyes as he left the room. If ever a man looked possessed of an evil spirit, it was he; but he did not speak. He walked down the stairs without a word, and then out into the street.

I stood and watched him until he was out of sight, and then tried to collect my scattered thoughts. On the whole, I was not pleased with the interview. I had shown my hand. It would have been far better if I could have allowed him still to think I was in his power, but the temptation to show him my freedom was too strong. It would now be a trial of skill between us. If he could have believed that I was unable to do anything to free myself, I should have, perhaps, caught him unawares. Now he would be prepared for everything I could do; he would check my every move. If Kaffar were alive, he would have a thousand means of keeping him out of my way; if dead—well, then, I did not care much what happened. If the latter, however, I determined to give up my life for Miss Forrest, to put myself in the hands of the police authorities, and tell of the influence Voltaire had exerted over me.

Meanwhile I must act, and that quickly; so I went straight to a private detective, a man I slightly knew. I refrained from going to Scotland Yard, as I thought Voltaire would be watching me. I gave this detective a description of Voltaire, told him his address, which I had ascertained through his letters to Temple Hall, and explained my wishes to him. He took up my points very quickly, saw what I wanted without any lengthened explanations, and expressed a willingness to serve me. So much pleased was I with this interview, that I had no fear that my enemy would not be well looked after.

After that I took train for Dover, and prepared to track Kaffar, if possible, wherever he had gone, not realizing at the time the task I had proposed for myself.

I thought I made a forward step at Dover, for, on inquiring at an hotel there, I found that a man answering to Kaffar's description had engaged a bedroom for one night, and had gone on to Calais by the midday boat, in time to catch the express for Paris.

"Did this gentleman have any luggage?" I asked.

The hotel proprietor did not think the gentleman carried any luggage, but he would inquire.

On inquiry of the hotel porter, I found that he carried a Gladstone bag, rather small and new. This was particularly remembered—first, because the foreign gentleman seemed very particular about it, and, second, because there seemed to be nothing in it.

So far so good.

I determined to go on to Paris; it could do no harm, it might do good. I could speak the French language fairly, and might, by some means, find out the steps he had taken.

Arrived at Paris, I was completely blocked. He was not remembered in the Custom House; he was not remembered at some twenty hotels at which I called.

Again I began to think what he was likely to do. I did not think he would possess very much money, and a man of his temperament would devise some means of getting some. How? Work would be a slow process, and not suited to his nature. Kaffar would get money by gambling. But that did not help me forward. To search out all the gambling-houses in Paris would be a hopeless task; besides, would he gamble in Paris, a city of which he knew nothing? I did not think so. Where, then?

Monte Carlo!

No doubt the reader will smile at my attempts as a private detective, but, realizing the circumstances by which I was surrounded, there may be some excuse for my unbusinesslike way of going to work. Besides, I was not sure that Kaffar was alive; I only had some vague grounds for thinking he was.

I went to Monte Carlo. I inquired at the hotels; I inquired at the Casino—without success. I learnt one great lesson there, however, and that was the evil of gambling. In spite of tinsel and gilt, in spite of gay attire and loud laughter, in spite of high-sounding titles and ancient names, never did I see so much real misery as I saw in the far-renowned gaming palace.

For days I tried to think what to do, without avail. Kaffar had not been at the Casino; he had not stayed at any of the hotels. Where was he, then?

I began to entertain the idea that he had gone to Egypt as he had said. I would do my best to find out. Accordingly, I went to all the seaports along the coast of France and Italy from which he would be likely to set sail for Egypt. I was unsuccessful until I came to Brindisi.

Here I found that inquiries could easily be made. There were only two hotels in the place, one of which was very small. At the smaller of the two, I found on inquiry that a man answering to my description had stayed there a day and a night, waiting for the boat for Alexandria. The hotel proprietor said he should not have remembered him, but that he had talked Arabic with him. This traveller had also told him he had come from England, the land of luxury and gold, and was going to Cairo.

He did not remember his name. Egyptians often came to Brindisi, and to him one name was pretty much like another. He called them all "Howajja," and remembered nothing more. He did not keep an hotel register.

Little and poor as this evidence was, I determined to go to Egypt. It was now June, and terribly hot, even at Brindisi; I knew the heat must be worse in Cairo, but that was nothing. If I could find this man, I should be rewarded a thousandfold.

Accordingly the next night, when an Austrian Lloyd steamer stopped at this little old-fashioned seaport on its way to Alexandria, I secured a berth and went on board. The voyage was not long, neither was it very tedious; at night, especially, it was glorious. To sit on deck and gaze at the smooth sea, which reflected in its deep waters the bright starry heavens, while the splash of the waters made music on the vessel's side, was to experience something not easily forgotten.

Arrived in Alexandria, I again set inquiries on foot, but with far less chance of success. Kaffar was not a marked man here. In this town, where almost every nationality was to be seen, no notice would be taken of him. A thousand men answering to Kaffar's description might be seen every day. Still I did all I could, and then hurried on to Cairo.

I have not tried to give any detailed account of my journeys, nor of the alternate feelings of hope and despair that possessed me. This must be left to the imagination of my readers. Let them remember the circumstances of the story as I have related them, let them think of how much depended on my discovery of Kaffar, let them also try to fancy something of my feelings, and then they will be able to guess at my weary nights and anxious days, they will know how feverishly I hurried from port to port and from town to town. Anyhow, I will not try to describe them, for I should miserably fail.

Cairo was comparatively empty. The heat had driven the tourists away to colder climes. The waiters in the hotels lolled around, with little or nothing to do. Only a few guests required their attendance. Everything was very quiet. The burning sun fairly scorched the leaves of the acacia trees, which grew everywhere. The Nile was exceedingly low, and water was comparatively scarce. The older part of Cairo was simply unbearable; the little Koptic community dwelling in the low huts, which reeked with dirt and vermin, would, one would have thought, have been glad to have died.

I had no success in Cairo. A dozen times I was buoyed up with hopes, a dozen times my hopes were destroyed, leaving me more despairing than ever. In spite of the terrible heat, all that could be done I did. Recommended by an hotel proprietor, I engaged two of the shrewdest men in this wonderful city to try and find Kaffar, but they could discover no trace of him. I went to mosques, to temples, to bazaars— in vain. If he were in Cairo, he was hiding.

Oh, the weary work, the dreadful uncertainty! Hoping, despairing, ever toiling, ever searching, yet never achieving! The months were slipping by. It was now August, and I was no nearer finding him than when I started. Must I give up, then? Should I renounce my life's love? Should I yield my darling to Voltaire? Never!

I formed a new resolution. I would go back to England. Doubtless I had gone clumsily to work, and thus my failure would be explained. When once back in London, I would engage the cleverest detectives the city could boast of, and I would state the whole case to them. Perchance they could do what I had failed to accomplish. This determination I at once carried into practice, and in a little more than a week I again saw the white cliffs of Dover. I did not rest. Arriving at Victoria, I drove straight to Scotland Yard, and in an hour later two of the most highly recommended officers of the London detective police force were in possession of all the facts that I could give them that would lead to the discovery of the Egyptian, providing he lived.

Then I drove back to my rooms in Gower Street, weary and sad, yet not hopeless. There were four months in which to act. Two clever men were at work, while, thank God, I was free to act and to think.

Yet the future looked terribly doubtful. Would the inquiries be successful? would Gertrude be freed from Voltaire? and should I be happy?

CHAPTER XVII

USING THE ENEMY'S WEAPONS

Two months passed, and no tidings of Kaffar—at least, none that were worthy of consideration. The detectives had done all that men could do; they had made every inquiry possible, they had set on foot dozens of schemes; but all in vain. Voltaire, who had been closely watched, was apparently living a quiet, harmless life, and was not, so far as could be seen, in communication with him. I had done all that I could do myself. I had followed in England every possible clue, all of which had ended in failure.

Three months passed. Still no reliable news. One detective fancied he had detected him in Constantinople; another was equally certain he had, at the same time, seen him in Berlin. I became almost mad with despair. The first of December had come, and I was not a step nearer finding the man whose presence would free me from Voltaire's villainous charge.

That which troubled me most was the fact that I did not know whether he were alive. Even if I did not kill him, perhaps Voltaire had got him out of the way so that he might fasten the guilt on me. "What, after all," was the thought that maddened me, "if he should be lying at the bottom of Drearwater Pond?"

There were only twenty-four days now. Three weeks and three days, and I knew not what to do. If I failed, my love would marry the man who was worse than a fiend, while I, for whom she was to suffer this torture, was unable to help her.

And yet I had tried, God alone knows how; but only to fail. Still, there were twenty-four days; but what were they? Kaffar, if he were alive, might be in Africa, Australia—no one knew where. I saw no hope.

A week more slipped by. There were only seventeen days left now. I was sitting in my room, anxiously waiting for the Continental mail, and any telegrams which might arrive. I heard the postman's knock, and in a minute more letters were brought in. Eagerly I opened those which came from the detectives, and feverishly read them. "Still in the dark; nothing discovered"—that summed up the long reports they sent me. I read the other letters; there was nothing in them to help me.

Still another week went by. Only ten days were wanting to Christmas Eve, and I knew no more of Kaffar's whereabouts than I did on the day when I defied Voltaire and started on my search. Again reports from the detectives came, and still no news. No doubt, by this, Voltaire was gloating over his victory, while I was nearly mad with despair.

Only ten days! I must do something. It was my duty, at all hazards, to free Gertrude Forrest from Voltaire. That was plain. I could not find the Egyptian, and thus it was probable I had killed him as had been said. What must I do? This, and this only. I must go to Scotland Yard, and relate to the authorities my whole story. I must tell them of Voltaire's influence over me, and that it was probable I had, while held under a mesmerist's spell, killed the man I had been trying to find. This was all. It *might* bring this villain under suspicion, and, if so, it would hinder him from exacting the fulfilment of Gertrude Forrest's promise.

It was at best but an uncertain venture, but it was all I could do. I owed it to the woman I loved. It was my duty to make this sacrifice. I would do it.

I wasted no time; I put on my overcoat and walked to Scotland Yard.

I put my hand upon the door of the room which I knew belonged to one of the officials, to whom I determined to report my case.

I thought of the words I should say, when—

"STOP!"

I am sure I heard that word, clear and distinct. Where it came from I knew not; but it was plain to me.

An idea flashed into my mind!

Mad, mad, I must have been, never to have thought of it before.

Ten days! Only ten days! But much might be done even yet. I rushed away, and got into St. James's Park, and there, in comparative quietness, I began to think.

The clouds began to dispel, the difficulties began to move away. Surely I had hit upon a plan at last, a plan on which I should have thought at the outset.

I walked on towards Westminster Abbey, still working out

my newly conceived idea, and when there jumped into a cab.

Yes, I remembered the address, for I had seen it only the day before, so I told the cabman to drive to—Street, Chelsea.

I was right. There on the door was the name of the man I had hoped to find—Professor Von Virchow. I paid the cabman, and knocked at the door with a beating heart.

A sallow-faced girl opened the door, and asked my business.

Was Professor Virchow at home?

Yes, he was at home, but would be engaged for the next quarter of an hour; after that, he could see me on business connected with his profession.

I was accordingly ushered into a musty room, which sadly wanted light and air. The quarter of an hour dragged slowly away, when the sallow-faced girl again appeared, saying that Professor Von Virchow would be pleased to see me.

I followed her into an apartment that was fitted up like a doctor's consulting-room. Here I found the man I had come to see.

He was a little man, about five feet four inches high. He had, however, a big head, a prominent forehead, and keen grey eyes. He wore gold-rimmed spectacles, and was evidently well fed and on good terms with himself.

"You are a professor of mesmerism and clairvoyance, I believe?" I began.

"That is my profession," said the little man, "Then I am in hopes that you may be able to help me in my difficulty."

"I shall be pleased to help you," he said, still stiffly.

"Can you," I went on, "tell the whereabouts of a man whom I may describe to you?"

"That is very vague," was the reply. "Your description may be incorrect, or a hundred men might answer to it. I would promise nothing under such conditions."

"Perhaps I had better tell my story," I said.

"I think you had," said the little professor, quietly.

"On the 2nd of January of the present year," I said, "a man disappeared in the night from a place in Yorkshire. He is an Egyptian, and easily distinguished. A great deal depends on finding him at once. Ever since May, endeavours have been made to track him, but without success."

"Perhaps he is dead," said the professor.

"Perhaps so; but even then it is important to know. Can you help me to find out his whereabouts?"

"Undoubtedly I can; but I must have a good photograph of him. Have you one?"

"I have not."

"Could you obtain one?"

"I think not."

"But this man has been seen by many people. Could not some one you know, and who knows him, sketch a faithful likeness from memory?"

"I do not know of any one."

"Then I could not guarantee to find him. You see, I cannot work miracles. I can only work through certain laws which I have been fortunate enough either to recognize or discover; but there must ever be some data upon which to go, and, you see, you give me none that is in the least satisfactory."

"Perhaps you can," I said, "if I relate to you all the circumstances connected with what is, I think, a somewhat remarkable story."

I had determined to tell this little man every circumstance which might lead to Kaffar's discovery, especially those which happened in Yorkshire. It seemed my only resource, and I felt, that somehow something would come of it.

I therefore briefly related what I have written in this story.

"That man who mesmerized you is very clever," said the professor quietly, when I had finished. "It was very unfortunate for you that you should have matched yourself with such a one. His plot was well worked out in every respect. He only made a mistake in one thing."

"And that?"

"He thought it impossible that you should ever be freed from his power without his consent. Still it was a well-planned affair. The story, the ghost, the quarrel—it was all well done."

"I fail to see what part the ghost had in the matter," I said.

The professor smiled. "No?" he said. "Well, I should not think it was a vital part of his plan, but it was helpful. He calculated upon the young lady's superstitious fancies. He knew what the particular form in which the ghost appeared portended, and it fitted in with his scheme of murder. Evidently he wanted the young lady to believe in your guilt, and thus give him greater chance of success. Ah, he is a clever man."

"But," I asked anxiously, "can you tell me Kaffar's whereabouts now?"

"No, I cannot—that is, not to-day."

"When, then?"

"I may not be able to do so at all. It all depends on one man."

"Who is he?"

"Simon Slowden, I think you called him."

"Simon Slowden! How can he help us?"

"Evidently he is susceptible to mesmeric influences, and he knows the man you wish to find. But the difficulty lies here. Is he sufficiently susceptible?"

"Is that the only hope?"

"All I can see at present. I was going to suggest that you be thrown into a mesmeric sleep; but you could not be depended on. The experiences which you have had would make you very uncertain."

"Then your advice is—"

"Send for this man at once. If he fails—well, I have another alternative."

"May I know what?"

"No, not now."

"Answer me this. Do you think I killed Kaffar, the Egyptian?"

"No, I do not; but your enemy intended you should."

"Why did I not, then?"

"Because the Egyptian also possessed a mesmerist's power, and hindered you. At any rate, such is my opinion. I am not sure;" and the little man looked very wise.

"Expect us early to-morrow morning," I said, and then went away to the nearest telegraph office, with a lighter heart than I had known for many long months. The little professor had given me some hope. The matter was still enshrouded in mystery, but still I thought I had found a possible solution.

"*Send Simon Slowden to me at once*" I telegraphed. "*Extremely important. Wire back immediately the time I may expect him.*"

Anxiously I waited for an answer. Although the message was flashed with lightning speed, it seemed a long time in coming. At length it came, and I read as follows:

"*Slowden will come by train leaving Leeds 11.38. Meet him at St. Pancras.*"

I immediately caught a cab and drove to Gower Street, and, on looking at my time-table, I found that the train mentioned in the telegram arrived in London at 5.15. This would do splendidly. I could get Simon to my room and give him some breakfast, and then, after a little rest, drive direct to the professor's.

I need not say I was early at St. Pancras the following morning. I had scarcely slept through the night, and anxiously awaited the appearance of the train. It swept into the station in good time, and, to my great relief and delight, I saw Simon appear on the platform, looking as stolid and imperturbable as ever.

We were not long in reaching Gower Street, where Simon enjoyed a good breakfast, after which we drew up our chairs before the cheerful fire and began to talk.

"Did you have a good journey, Simon?" I asked.

"Slept like the seven sleepers of the patriarch, sur, all the way from Leeds."

"And you don't feel tired now?"

"Not a bit, yer honour."

"Then," I said, "I want to explain to you a few things that must have appeared strange."

Accordingly I told him of Voltaire's influence over me, and what came out of it.

"Why, sur," said Simon, when I had finished, "that 'ere willain must be wuss nor a hinfidel; he must be the Old Nick in the garret. And do you mean to say, sur, that that 'ere beautiful Miss Forrest, who I've put down for you, is goin' to git married to that 'ere somnamblifyin' waccinatin' willain, if his dutiful mate ain't a found before Christmas Eve?"

"Only nine days, Simon."

"But it mustn't be, yer honour."

"So I say, Simon; and that's why I've sent for you."

"But I can't do nothink much, sur. All my wits hev bin waccinated away, and my blood is puddled like, which hev affected the workin' o' my brains; and, you see, all your detective chaps have failed."

"But I shan't fail, if you'll help me."

"Help you, Mr. Blake? You know I will!"

"Simon, you offered to be my friend, now nearly a year ago."

"Ay, and this 'ere is a lad as'll stick to his offer, sur, and mighty proud to do so."

"Well, then, I'm in hopes we shall succeed."

"How, yer honour?"

"By fighting Voltaire with his own weapons."

"What, waccinatin'?"

"By mesmerism and clairvoyance, Simon."

"And who's the chap as hev got to be waccinated—or mesmerized, as you call it?"

"You, if you will, Simon."

"Me, sir?" said Simon, aghast.

"If you will."

"Well, I said after that 'ere willain experimented on me in Yorkshire, I never would again; but if it's for you, sur—why, here goes; I'm purty tough. But how's it to be done?"

Then I told him of my interview with the professor, and how he had told me that only he—Simon—could give the necessary help.

"Let's off at once, yer honour," cried Simon. "I'm willin' for anything if you can git the hupper 'and of that 'ere willain and his other self. Nine days, sur—only nine days! Let's git to the waccinator. I'd rather have small-pox a dozen times than you should be knocked overboard by sich as he."

I was nothing loth, and so, although it was still early, we were soon in a cab on our way to the professor's. On arriving, we were immediately shown in, and the little man soon made his appearance.

"Ah! you've brought him?" said he. "I'm glad to see you so prompt. Would you mind taking this chair, my friend?"—to Simon. "That's it, thank you. You've been travelling all night and are a little tired, I expect. No? Well, it's well to be strong and able to bear fatigue. There, look at me. Ah, that's it!"

With that he put his fingers on Simon's forehead, and my humble friend was unconscious of what was going on around him.

"He's very susceptible; but I am afraid he has not been under this influence a sufficient number of times for his vision to be clear. Still, we'll try.—Simon!"

"That's me," said Simon, sleepily.

"Do you see Kaffar, the Egyptian?"

He looked around as if in doubt. His eyes had a vacant look about them, and yet there seemed a certain amount of intelligence displayed—at any rate, it seemed so to me.

"I see lots of people, all dim like," said Simon, slowly; "but I can't tell no faces. They all seem to be covered wi' a kind o' mist."

"Look again," said the professor. "You can see more clearly now."

Simon peered again and again, and then said, "Yes, I can see him; but he looks all strange. He's a-shaved off his whiskers, and hev got a sort o' red cap, like a baisin, on his head."

My heart gave a great bound. Kaffar was not dead. Thank God for that!

"Where is he?"

"I am tryin' to see, but I can't. Everything is misty. There's a black fog a-comin' up."

"Wait a few minutes," said the professor, "and then we'll try him again."

Presently he spoke again. "Now," he said, "what do you see?"

But Simon did not reply. He appeared in a deep sleep.

"I thought as much," said the little man. "His nature has not been sufficiently prepared for such work. I suppose you had breakfast before you came here?"

I assured him that Simon had breakfasted on kidneys and bacon; after which he had made considerable inroads into a cold chicken, with perchance half a pound of cold ham to keep it company. Besides which, he had taken three large breakfast cups of chocolate.

"Ah, that explains somewhat. Still, I think we have done a fair morning's work. We've seen that our man is alive."

"But do you think there is any hope of finding him?"

"I'm sure there is, only be patient."

"But what must I do?"

"Well, take this man to see some of the sights of London until three o'clock, then come home to dinner. After dinner he'll be sleepy. Let him sleep, if he will, until nine o'clock; then bring him here again; but let him have no supper until after I have done with him."

"Nine o'clock to-night! Why, do you know, that takes away another day? There will only want eight clear days to Christmas Eve."

"I can't help that, sir," said the little professor, testily; "you should have come before. But that is the way. Our science, which is really the queen of sciences, is disregarded; only one here and there comes to us, and then we are treated as no other scientific man would be treated. Never mind, our day will come. One day all the sciences shall bow the knee to us, for we are the real interpreters of the mysteries of nature."

I apologized for my impatience, which he gravely accepted, and then woke Simon from his sleep.

"Where am I?" cried Simon. "Where've I been?"

"I can't tell," said the professor; "I wish I could, for then our work would be accomplished."

"Have you bin a-waccinatin' me?" said Simon.

The little man looked to me for explanation.

"He calls everything mysterious by that name," I said.

"'Cause," continued Simon, "I thought as how you waccinators, or mesmerists, made passes, as they call 'em, and waved your hands about, and like that."

"Did that Mr. Voltaire, I think you call him, make passes?" asked the professor.

"He!" said Simon. "He ain't no ordinary man. He's got dealin's with old Nick, he hev. He didn't come near me, nor touch me, and I wur sleepin' afore I could think of my grandmother."

"Just so; he is no ordinary man. He's a real student of psychology, he is. He has gone beyond the elements of our profession. I despise the foolish things which these quacks of mesmerism make Billy people do in order to please a gaping-mouthed audience. It is true I call myself a professor of mesmerism and clairvoyance, but it would be more correct to call me a practical psychologist. You'll attend to my wishes with regard to our friend, won't you? Good-morning."

I will not try to describe how I passed the day. It would be wearisome to the reader to tell him how often I looked at my watch and thought of the precious hours that were flying;

neither will I speak of my hopes and fears with regard to this idea of finding Kaffar's whereabouts by means of clairvoyance. Suffice it to say I was in a state of feverish anxiety when we drove up to the professor's door that night, about half-past nine.

We did not wait a minute before operations were commenced. Simon was again in a mesmeric sleep, or whatever the reader may be pleased to call it, in a few seconds after he had sat down.

Von Virchow began by asking the same question he had asked in the morning: "Do you see Kaffar, the Egyptian?"

I waited in breathless silence for the answer. Simon heaved a deep sigh, and peered wearily around, while the professor kept his eye steadily upon him.

"Do you see Kaffar, the Egyptian?" repeated he.

"Yes, I see him," said Simon at length.

"Where?"

"That's what I'm trying to find out," said Simon. "The place is strange; the people talk in a strange tongue. I can't make 'em out."

"What do you see now?" said the professor, touching his forehead.

"Oh, ah, I see now," said Simon. "It's a railway station, and I see that 'ere willain there, jest as cunnin' as ever. He's a gettin' in the train, he is."

"Can you see the name of the station?"

"No, I can't. It's a biggish place it is, and I can't see no name. Stay a minute, though. I see now."

"Well, what's the name?"

"It's a name as I never see or heard tell on before. B-O-L-O—ah, that's it; BOLOGNA, that's it. It is a queer name though, ain't it?"

"Well, what now?"

"Why, he's in the train, and it's started, it is."

"Do you know where he's going?"

"No."

"But he has a ticket; can't you see it?"

"Course I can't. It's in his pocket, and I can't see through the cloth, I can't."

"And what's he doing now?"

"Why, he's in for makin' hisself comfortable, he is. He's got a piller, and he's stretchin' hisself on the seat and layin' his head on the piller. There, he's closed his eyes—he's off to sleep."

The professor turned to me. "I am afraid we can do no more to-night," he said. "Evidently he is on a journey, and we must wait until he arrives at his destination."

"But can't Slowden remain as he is and watch him?"

"The thing would be at once cruel and preposterous, sir. No, you must come again in the morning; then, perchance, he will have finished his journey;" and accordingly he proceeded to awake Simon.

After all, it did not matter so much. It was now ten o'clock, and I could do nothing that night, in any case.

"I do not know but that I am glad that things are as they are," continued the professor. "This second sleep will enable him to see more clearly to-morrow. Meanwhile, consider yourself fortunate. If the Egyptian stops anywhere in Italy, it will be possible for you to reach him and bring him back within the time you mention. Take heart, my friend. Good-bye for the time. I shall expect you early to-morrow."

No sooner were we in the street than Simon began to ask me what he had told me, for I found that he was entirely ignorant of the things he had said.

"Who'd 'a thought it?" he said musingly, when I had told him. "Who'd 'a thought as 'ow I should hassist in a waccinatin' business like this 'ere! Tell 'ee, yer 'onour, I shall believe in ghosts and sperrits again soon. Fancy me a-seein' things in Italy and tellin' 'em to you without knowin' anything about it! Well, but 'twill be grand if we can find 'im, yer honour, won't it then?"

I spent a sleepless night, harassed by a thousand doubts and fears. There, in the quiet of my room, all this mesmerism and clairvoyance seemed only so much hocus-pocus, which no sensible and well-educated man should have anything to do with. Still, it was my only hope, and it only wanted eight days to Christmas Eve. Only one little week and a day, that was all, and then, if I did not produce Kaffar, all was lost. It would be no use to go to Miss Forrest's house in Kensington and tell her that Simon Slowden had, while in a mesmeric sleep, seen Kaffar in Italy. No, no; that would never do. I must produce him, nothing else would suffice.

We were early at the professor's the following morning, and found him waiting and almost as anxious as we were. Again Simon submitted to the influence of the little man, and soon answered his questions far more readily than he had hitherto done.

Did he see Kaffar?

"Yes," was the reply.

"Where is he now?"

He was in a beautiful town. The houses were white, the streets were white; the town was full of squares, and in these squares were many statues. Such was Simon's information.

"Do you know what country the town is in?"

"No," said Simon, shaking his head.

"Could you not by any means find out? There's a railway station in the town; can you not see the name there?"

"Yes, there's a railway station, a fine one. Ah, I see the name now. T-O-R-I-N-O. TORINO, that's it."

"Torino!" I cried, "Turin! That's a town in Italy, some distance beyond the French border."

The professor beckoned me to be quiet.

"Kaffar is at Torino, is he?" said the professor.

"That's it—yes."

"What is he doing?"

"Talkin' with a man who keeps an hotel."

"What does he say?"

"It's in a foreign language, and I can't tell."

"Can you repeat what he said?"

"It sounded like this—'*Je restey ici pour kelka jour*;' but I can't make out what it means."

The professor turned to me.

"He's speaking French. I did not know Kaffar knew French; perhaps he's learned it lately. The words mean that he will stay there for some days."

"Can you describe the street in which this hotel is?" continued Von Virchow.

Simon began to describe, but we could make nothing of it.

"We can't understand," replied the professor. "Can you draw a sketch of the road to it from the railway station?" and he put a piece of paper and pencil in Simon's hand.

Without hesitating, Simon drew a sketch, a facsimile of which is given on the opposite page.

I had been to Turin, and remembered some of the places the sketch indicated. It might be far from perfect, but it was sufficient for me. It would be child's play to find Kaffar there.

"That will do," I said to the professor. "I'll start at once. Thank you so much."

"Ah, that will do, will it?" he said, with a smile. "Then I'll wake up this man."

Simon woke up as usual, rubbing his eyes, and asked whether any good had been done.

"Everything's been done," cried I. "Come, professor, allow me to write you a cheque. How much shall it be?"

"Not a penny until your work is accomplished," replied the little man, with dignity.

"That is not fair," I said. "I don't know what may happen, and you must not be defrauded. Anyhow, here's something on account;" and I put a twenty-pound note in his hand.

He smiled as he looked at it, while I took my hat, and stated my intention to start for Turin at once.

"Beggin' yer pardon," said Simon, "but this 'ere waccination business is awfully wearyin', and I should like to—that is—"

"The very thing," I replied, anticipating his request. "You shall go with me."

Half-an-hour later, we were at Gower Street, making preparations for our journey to Turin—Simon calm and collected, I feverish and excited.

CHAPTER XVIII

NEARING THE END

There were, as I said, eight days in which to find Kaffar and bring him to London, counting the day on which we started our journey. It was Wednesday; by the following Wednesday, at midnight, I must prove to Gertrude that Voltaire was a villain and a liar. It should be done easily. It was but little more than a thirty hours' ride to Turin—that is, providing everything went smoothly. To put it at the outside, it was only a forty-eight hours' journey, allowing time for a sleep on the way. Thus four days would suffice for travelling, and I should have more than three days in which to find Kaffar. It was true Turin was a large town, but in three days I was sure I could find him. In that time I thought I could hunt every lodging-house and hotel in the city.

I shall say little of the journey. Mostly it was cold and wearisome enough. From Dover to Paris it was fairly comfortable, but from Paris to the Italian border we were travelling through a snowstorm, and thus, when we came to this our last stopping-place before going through the famous Mont Cenis Tunnel, we were four hours late. It was terribly cold there. Everything was ice-bound. Brooklets, waterfalls, rivers, all were held fast by the ice-king. Simon was much impressed by the scenery. The great giant mountains towering up on every hand were a revelation to him, and he stood open-mouthed, gazing at what is perhaps among the grandest sights in France.

We swept through Mont Cenis Tunnel, and then, with a cry of gladness, we entered the sunny land of Italy. What a change it was! Here the warm sun, which had been hidden on the other side by the high mountain range, had melted the snow, and so bright streams of water came rushing down the mountain sides, laughing as if in glee. The cottagers sat outside their doors, singing in the sun. The vine-covered hills, although not yet clothed with their green garment, were still beautiful, while away in the distance spread a broad Italian plain, dotted with villages, out of whose midst a modest church spire ever lifted its head.

I had seen all this before, but to Simon it was a marvel of beauty. In England the streets were muddy, and a yellow fog hung over London, and yet in forty-eight hours we were beneath sunny skies, we were breathing a comparatively humid air.

But I must not stay to write about this, for my story is not about Italian scenery, or beautiful sights of any sort. It is my work now to tell about my search after Kaffar.

We arrived in Turin on Friday evening, about fifty-one hours from the time we started from London. We had spent some little time in Paris, or we could have done it more quickly. We found Turin lit up with a pure bright light, and, as Simon declared, "looking one of the most purtiest places like, as ever he'd clapped his eyes on."

We stayed at Hotel Trombetta. We had several reasons for doing this. First, it was a good hotel. I had stayed there before, and so I knew. It was also near the station, and fairly near the place where, according to Simon's sketch, Kaffar was staying. We got into the hotel just in time for dinner. Simon declared that he "dar'n't go into the dining-room amo' the swells like; it would take away his appetite jist like waccination did;" but as I insisted, he gave way, and certainly did not draw any one's attention by his awkwardness. I had got him a perfectly fitting suit of clothes in Paris, in which he looked a respectable member of society.

Directly after dinner I went out, to try to find Kaffar's whereabouts; but although Turin is beautifully built, and the streets very straight, I found I had to put off my search until the morning.

Every hour of waiting was, as the reader may imagine, of great anxiety to me. I was now making my great move. If I missed in this, all was lost. Was Kaffar in Turin? Was he or had he been there? Was all this mesmerism so much hocus-pocus and nonsense to deceive me, a credulous fool? And yet I was sure Simon would not be a party in deceiving me. But might not I have been deceived by the professor? Could he not make my friend say, not what really existed, but what existed in his own mind? And yet the little man seemed honest! Anyhow, I could do no more, and it was my only hope. There could be no harm in trying. If I failed, well, I could not help it; I had done my best. I would go back and face Voltaire and Miss Forrest, and—well—I knew not what—! But if I found the Egyptian! Ah, it was too good to be true. I dared not dwell upon the thought. It was not for me to build castles in the air, and weave bright fancies; but to work, until I had accomplished the work I had set out to do.

And so I went quietly to bed, and, much to my astonishment, slept long and soundly. The sun was shining in at my window when I awoke, and this Italian city looked wondrously beautiful as it lay there this clear December morning, in the light of the bright sun.

We wasted no time after breakfast before setting out—I with beating heart, Simon still calm and collected, looking with critical eyes on the sketch he had drawn in his mesmeric sleep.

"After all," remarked Simon, slowly, "it shows us how a feller can live away from his body, don't it, then? We are fearfully and terribly made, as Solomon said to the people on Mount Sinai."

I did not reply to Simon's philosophy, nor to his wonderful scriptural quotations. I was too anxious to get to this hotel, where I hoped Kaffar would be staying.

We came to the great square in which stood the palace of the king, but I paid no heed to the imposing building nor to the magnificently carved monuments that stood around in the square. I was too anxious to turn down the street in which my hopes lay.

I went slowly down, till I came to the bottom of it, where a narrow road branched off, leading to a kind of observatory; but I saw nothing of an hotel.

My heart became like lead.

Simon's sketch of the streets had not been a false one. If any of my readers have been to Turin, they will remember the long street leading from the station; they will also recognize the two squares which Simon indicated in his plan. True, he had sketched them out of proportion, while the street was far more straight than he had drawn it. Still, it bore a close resemblance to that particular part of the city.

But there was no hotel, nor sign of one in the street.

We walked up and down again and again, with no success. Could it be that I had come all these weary miles again only for a bitter and terrible disappointment? The thought almost drove me mad.

I would not give up, however! There might be no hotel, but it was possible Kaffar stayed in a lodging-house, or even in a private house. I would knock at every house in the street, and make inquiries, before I would give up.

The Italian language was not altogether strange to me. I could not by any means speak it fluently, but I knew it enough to enter into an ordinary conversation. So, seeing a soldier pass up the street, I saluted him and asked him whether he knew a lodging-house or private boarding establishment in the street?

No, the soldier said, he did not know any at all in that street, or, indeed, in that part of the town; but if I would go with him, he would direct me to a splendid place, marvellously convenient, marvellously clean, and marvellously cheap, and, best of all, kept by his mother's sister.

I cannot say I felt either elated or depressed by this answer. Evidently this was a keen youth, trying to get a suitable customer for his relations.

Another youth came up to me soon after, offering to sell me photographs of some of the principal sights in Turin. Could he tell me of any boarding or lodging establishment in the street?

Yes, he knew of three or four. For a franc he would give me their history and lead me to them.

Was there one about the middle of the street?

Yes, there were two close together. Should he take me?

I closed with the youth's offer, and accordingly we walked down the street together. He entered a tobacconist's shop, assuring me that this was a lodging-house.

A young Italian girl stood behind the counter, as if waiting for an order; so I asked to see the proprietor of the place.

She immediately went out of the shop and gave a shout, and a minute after a matronly woman entered, about fifty years of age, and who, from her close resemblance to the dark-eyed girl, was probably her mother.

Was she the proprietor of this establishment?

She was.

Did she keep a boarding-house?

She did—for well-behaved people.

She had no husband?

The Blessed Virgin had taken him home.

And a man did not conduct her business?

Certainly not. She was a capable woman, able to attend to the wants of her guests, while her daughter was a universal favourite because of politeness to customers and the good tobacco she sold. Should she have the pleasure of selling me some?

I did not reply except by a smile, which this Italian maiden evidently took for an assent to her mother's proposition, and accordingly proceeded to make some cigarettes for me. Meanwhile her mother assured me that her house was convenient and comfortable, and asked permission to show me some vacant rooms, and give me an idea of the attendance I should receive.

I accordingly followed her, and found rooms which, while not altogether according to my English tastes, did her credit.

"Have you many lodgers now?" I asked.

"Four," was the reply.

"Gentlemen?"

"All gentlemen."

"Might I ask their nationality?" I said.

"They are all Italian," was the reply.

My hopes had risen high, but they were by this answer dashed to the ground. Then I remembered that Simon had described Kaffar as being in a room with a man. So, after thanking the lady for her kindness and paying for the cigarettes, I asked the boy, who was waiting for his franc, to show me to the other lodging-house close by.

"Oh, sir," said the proprietress of this establishment, "don't go there! It's a bad house; it really is! The lodgers are bad men, and they are bad people." She said this evidently in earnest, while the little girl behind the counter hoped I should not go among those thieves.

I was not displeased at this. I did not think Kaffar would be very particular as to his society, and he would be more likely to stay at this disreputable place than in a respectable lodging-house.

Accordingly, I told the good lady that I should not take lodgings there, and, if I took apartments in any place in the city, hers should have the first consideration. This considerably mollified her, so my guide proceeded to lead the way to the other lodging-house. This was also a tobacconist's shop, but a dirty old woman stood behind the counter. She was very polite, however, and quickly called down the proprietor of the establishment.

This was a lodging-house, was it not?

He assured me that my surmise was correct, and forthwith began to enumerate the advantages received by those who were fortunate enough to be received as lodgers.

"Have you many lodgers at present?" I asked.

"Five," was the reply.

My heart began to beat violently now, for I felt I was near the time when my labours would be rewarded by success, or I should have to give up my search in despair.

"Are they all Europeans?" I asked.

"No. There was one Turk, one Frenchman, two Italians, and one Egyptian."

My heart gave a great bound. Surely I had been guided aright; I should find him at last.

"Are they at home during the day?"

"No," was the reply; "they are mostly out."

"But they come home at night?"

"Yes, they come home at night, all except one."

Which was he?

The Egyptian.

Did he stay at home during the day?

He really could not say. He only came a little more than two days ago, and his habits seemed uncertain.

"And is the Egyptian at home now?"

"No," said the man, eyeing me keenly.

"Might I ask when he will be home?" I asked eagerly.

"I do not think it right to answer questions about my lodgers," said the man, sharply. "You have asked a great many; I must know your reasons for so doing before I answer any more."

I began to chide myself for my folly. I had raised suspicions, and now I might not be able to get the information I wanted. "I did not intend to be offensive," I said. "If I mistake not, this Egyptian gentleman is acquainted with a man in England whom I know, and I have a message of great importance to convey."

"To Mr. Kaffar's advantage?" asked the Italian, eagerly.

No words can express what I felt as the man unthinkingly uttered Kaffar's name. I had not come on a false report. The Egyptian bore the name of the man I wanted to find.

"He can turn it to his advantage," I replied.

"Mr. Kaffar is not in Turin at present," he said confidentially.

"Could you tell me where he is?" I said, with beating heart.

"I cannot. You see—" and the Italian put his face close to mine. "Might I ask if you are somewhat of a—well, a gentleman fond of play?"

I did not reply.

"Ah, I thought so," said he, cunningly. "At first I was afraid you were a detective fellow, but I see now. Well, you will perhaps know that Mr. Kaffar is a very accomplished gentleman, and he left yesterday afternoon for a little tour— where I don't know. Another accomplished gentleman went with him. We have a jolly house, and you Englishmen would enjoy a few nights here. Come up to-night and win some of our Italian gold."

"When will Mr. Kaffar be back?"

"He said he might be back on Monday night—on Tuesday morning at latest."

"I daren't come and play till he comes," I said. "Will he let you know when he is coming back?"

"Yes; he said he'd telegraph."

"Would you mind letting me know the train? I am staying at

the Hotel Trombetta."

"Yes, yes, I shall be delighted; and then, when he comes, we'll—But what name shall I write on my message?"

"Herod Voltaire," I said.

I went away then, and began to think. I found the man, and yet I had not. Nothing was certain yet. It was now Saturday, and he would not return until Monday night or Tuesday morning, and I must be in London by Wednesday at midnight, or all was lost. Say he came back on Tuesday by noon, there would then be only thirty-six hours left in which to get to London. Thirty-six hours, and many hundreds of dreary, weary miles between! Or if he should not come at all! If the Italian were deceiving me!

I shall not try and relate what happened the next two days, except to say that I set Simon to watch every train that came into Turin station, while I did all I could to discover whether he were hiding in Turin.

Neither of us saw Kaffar, nor did we hear anything of him.

Monday night came. I had received no message from the lodging-house keeper, neither had I heard any news. The suspense was becoming terrible.

Six o'clock! Seven o'clock, and no news!

"Simon," I said, "go to that lodging-house and ask whether any message has been received."

The willing fellow, still with a smile on his face and a cheery look, started to do my bidding. I do not know how I should have borne up during those two terrible days, but for my faithful friend.

He had not been gone above half a minute before he came bounding back to my room.

"A message jist 'a come, yer honour!" he cried.

Eagerly I snatched it, and read—"*Expect me home to-night by the midnight train.—KAFFAR.*"

I caught up a time-table and anxiously scanned it. The telegram was from *Nice*. There was a train due from this fashionable seaport at 12.30.

The lodging-house keeper had kept his word, and Kaffar would be safe. It was become intensely real, intensely exciting!

Five hours to wait—five hours! Only those who have felt as I did can know what they meant.

At twelve o'clock I sent Simon to the station, while I went to the lodging-house to await Kaffar's arrival.

"Mr. Kaffar will have supper, I suppose?" I said to the proprietor of the house.

"Yes, I shall prepare supper."

"Where?"

"In his own room."

"Just so. Could you manage to put me in a room where I can see him at supper without being observed? I should like to enter quietly and give him a surprise."

"You mean nothing wrong?"

"On my honour, I do not."

"It is said," mused the Italian, "that an English gentleman's honour is like English cloth; it can always be depended on. The adjoining room is empty, sir."

"Thank you," I replied, while he led the way to the room.

I had not been there long before I heard some one enter with the landlord. The two rooms, like many we find in French hotels, could easily be made one, as a doorway led from one to the other. I had arranged my door to be slightly ajar, so was able to see.

The man with the landlord was Kaffar!

I found that Kaffar could not speak Italian. He spoke French enough to make himself understood, and, as his host was proficient in that language, French was the tongue in which they conversed.

"Has any one been asking for me?" asked Kaffar.

"Yes, sir."

"Who?"

"A gentleman from England."

"From England! What kind of a man?"

"A giant, with brown hair."

"A giant, with brown hair! Man, where is he now?"

"How can I say?" said the Italian.

Kaffar held down his head for a minute, and then said hastily, "And his message?"

"Something to your advantage, sir."

"My advantage? Can it be he? Did he give his name?"

"Herod Voltaire!"

"Voltaire! Never! He dare not come near me; I'm his master for many reasons—he dare not come! But—"

He checked himself, as if he were telling the Italian too much. The host then left the room, while Kaffar went on with his supper.

I opened the door noiselessly and went into the room, and said distinctly, "Good evening, Mr. Kaffar."

He looked up and saw me. Never, I think, did I see so much terror, astonishment, mingled with hate, expressed on a human face before.

He made a leap for the door. I caught him, and held him fast.

"No, Mr. Kaffar, you must not escape," I said, leading him back to his chair.

"You cannot—kill me—here!" he gasped. "I mean no wrong—to you. I—Ah, you've followed me for revenge."

For an answer I went to the door and locked it.

"Have mercy!" he said. "Don't kill me. I—you don't know

all! Voltaire's your enemy, not I."

"You knew I was following you, did you?" I said.

"Yes. Voltaire said you were mad for my life; that you swore to be revenged; that you would pull me limb from limb! Ah, you do not know."

Surely I had found out the man's nature. He was a coward, and stood in deadly fear of me. He had been Voltaire's tool, who had frightened him to do his every bidding. Now I must use his fear of me to make him do my will.

"Well, I have found you out," I said. "You thought you would master me, didn't you?"

"Well, I'm master of you both. Voltaire's influence over me is gone, and now he is in my power; while you—"

"Ah, Mr. Blake, have mercy," he whined. "I only did what he told me, and he has treated me like a dog."

"Yes; he intended me to kill you, while both of you tried to ruin me."

"Curse him! I know he did. Oh, I am not his friend now. Mr. Blake, forgive me. Ah, say—"

I felt that if I allowed this man to think my welfare depended on his doing my will, he would defy me. I must use means suitable to the man.

"Kaffar," I said, "had I a heart like you Egyptians, you know what I should do; but—well, I will be merciful on one condition."

"Oh, what-what?"

"That you will come back to England with me at once."

"I cannot; I dare not. He has promised to take my life-blood if I do."

"No harm shall happen to you, I promise."

"You will not allow him to touch me?"

"He shall not."

"Then I will go."

My point was gained. The man had promised to accompany me willingly, while I had expected a difficult matter in getting him to England.

Early the next day we were on our way to England, Simon and I taking turns in watching the wily Egyptian.

CHAPTER XIX

THE SECOND CHRISTMAS EVE

The skies were clear when we left Turin, and the air pure and free. We had not got far into France, however, when we found everything changed. It was snow—snow everywhere. On ordinary occasions I should not have minded much, but now everything depended on my getting to London at a certain hour. How slowly the train seemed to creep, to be sure; and how long we stopped at the little roadside stations!

Simon did his best to cheer me, while Kaffar furtively watched us both, as if in fear. I was silent and fearful, for I felt sure the Egyptian meditated escape. The laughter of the light-hearted French people, who were preparing for Christmas festivities, grated on my ears; for, although I had succeeded almost beyond my hopes, a great fear rested upon me that I should fail even yet. Especially was this realized when I knew that our train was hours late, and I knew that did we not arrive in Paris at something like reasonable time, we should miss the express trains for England.

When we got to the French metropolis we were nearly five hours late. It was not to be wondered at, for the snow fell in blinding drifts, until, in some cases, the railways were completely blocked. The wonder was how we got to Paris so soon, when we considered what had to be contended with.

Anxiously I inquired after trains by which I could catch the boats for England, but the replies were vague. First, it was now Christmas Eve, which at all times caused the general traffic to be delayed; and, second, the weather was so bad that to state times of arrival was impossible.

It was now Wednesday morning, and I started from Paris with sixteen hours before me in which to get to London. Ordinarily I should have had time enough and to spare, but everything was delayed and confused. I had thought of going back by Dieppe and Newhaven; but a storm was blowing, and I knew that meant a longer sea-passage, so I went to Calais, thus riding through one of the most uninteresting parts of France. It was five o'clock on Christmas Eve when we arrived at this little French seaport, and then it took us two hours to cross the straits, although we happened to be on one of the fast-sailing steamers. We had now five hours to get to Kensington. I was getting terribly anxious now. If there should be a breakdown, or if anything should happen to hinder us! We were so near, and yet so far. Once I thought of telegraphing and telling of my success, but I refrained from that. I wanted to tell of my victory in person, and thus, if needs be, destroy Voltaire's last hope.

The usual time for an express train to run from Dover to Victoria is about two hours; but it was Christmas Eve, special trains were running, and passengers crowded on every hand, thus we were more than three hours in accomplishing the journey. The train swept into Victoria at a quarter-past ten. There was one hour and three-quarters to go to Kensington.

"This way to the Custom House," shouted one of the officials. I had forgotten this part of the programme, but I determined not to wait for my luggage. I would sooner lose it a thousand times over than be late in reaching Kensington. I accordingly got the keys from Kaffar and Simon, and pointing out the portmanteaus to an official, gave him a sovereign to see them examined and sent on to my address in Gower Street.

I hailed a hansom, but the cabby refused to take the three of us, upon which Kaffar offered to go in another; but I dared not risk him out of my sight, so we got into a rumbling old four-wheeler, and I offered the cabby a sovereign if he would get me at the address I gave him in half-an-hour.

"Couldn't do it for ten sovereigns, sir," said the cabby. "The streets is as slippery as glass, and as crowded as herrin's in a barrel. I'll do it in *three-quarters* for a quid, yer honour."

It was now nearly half-past ten; that would make it a quarter-past eleven. To me it was drawing it terribly fine, but I consented. If he were not spurred on by thought of reward, short as the distance was, there was no knowing how long he would be.

At length the cab stopped. It was a quarter-past eleven, and as I got out I noticed that we stood in front of one of those tall noble-looking mansions which are so common in Kensington.

"Wait a minute," I said to the cabby; "I want to be certain this is the right house." Meanwhile I noticed that my constant friend Simon held Kaffar by the arm.

I rang the bell violently, and a servant appeared at the door.

Did Miss Gertrude Forrest live there?

Yes.

Was she at home?

Yes.

Could I see her?

The servant was not sure, but would ascertain. Miss Forrest was then engaged.

I stopped the man, for I did not wish to appear in the way that matters seemed to promise. Meanwhile Simon had paid the cabby, and so the three of us stood together in the hall.

"I am an old friend of Miss Forrest's," I said to the man; "I want to be shown to the room where she is, without her being apprised of my presence."

"I daren't," he replied; "it would be as much as my place is worth."

"No, it would not," I replied. "You would not suffer in the slightest degree."

"But there are several people in the room," he said, eyeing a sovereign I was turning over in my hand.

"How many?"

"There's Miss Forrest, her aunt, and Miss Staggles, besides a gentleman that came early in the evening."

"That gentleman's name is Herod Voltaire," I said.

"Yes, sir, that's the name. Well, I'll do as you wish me."

I followed the servant, while Simon kept fast hold on Kaffar. The man knocked at the door, while I stood close behind him, and the moment he opened the door I entered the room.

Never shall I forget the sight. Evidently Voltaire had been claiming the fulfilment of her promise, for he was earnestly speaking when I entered, while Miss Forrest, pale as death, sat by an elderly lady, who I concluded to be her aunt. Miss Staggles also sat near, as grim and taciturn as ever.

"It is nearly twelve o'clock," I heard Voltaire say, "and he's not here. He dare not come; how dare he? He has left the country, and will never return again."

"But I am here," I said distinctly.

They all turned as I spoke, and Miss Forrest gave a scream. I had been travelling incessantly for forty hours, so I am afraid I did not present a very pleasant appearance. No doubt I was travel-stained and dusty enough.

"Who are you?" demanded Voltaire.

"You know well enough who I am," I said.

"Begone!" he cried; "this is no place for murderers."

"No," I said, "it is not."

No sooner had Miss Forrest realized who I was, than she rushed to my side.

"Oh, are you safe—are you safe?" she said huskily.

I looked at her face, and it was deathly pale, while her eyes told me she had passed sleepless nights.

"No, he's not safe," said Voltaire, "and he shall pay for this with his life."

"Is it manly," I said to him, "to persecute a lady thus? Can't you see how she scorns you, hates you, loathes you? Will you insist on her abiding by a promise which was made in excitement to save an innocent man?"

"Innocent!" he sneered, and I noticed a look of victory still in his glittering eye. "Innocent! Yes, as innocent as Nero or Robespierre; but you shall not come here to pollute the air by your presence. Begone! before I forget myself, and send for the police to lock you up. Ah, I long for vengeance on the man who murdered my dear friend."

"Then you will not release Miss Forrest?"

"Never!"

"Then I shall make you."

"You make me?" he cried savagely.

Meanwhile Miss Forrest had clung tremblingly to my arm; Miss Forrest's aunt had looked fearfully, first at Voltaire, then at me; while Miss Staggles had been mumbling something about showing me out of doors.

"Yes," I said; "I shall make you."

"You cannot," he jeered. "I have it in my power now to lodge you safe in a felon's gaol, and bring you to a hangman's noose."

"Ay, and I would too," cried Miss Staggles. "You are too kind, too forbearing, Mr. Voltaire."

"Oh, leave me," cried Miss Forrest, clinging closer to me; "I will suffer anything rather than you should be—be—"

"Ring the bell for a servant," I said; and Miss Forrest's aunt tremblingly touched a button close beside her.

The man who had showed me in immediately answered the summons.

"Show my friends in," I said.

A minute more and Simon entered, carefully leading Kaffar. Voltaire gave a yell like that of a mad dog, while Miss Forrest gave a scream of delight.

"There, villain," I said, "is the man whom you say I've murdered."

"How dare you come here?" said Voltaire to Kaffar.

"Because I brought him," I said, "to save this lady and expose you. Now, where is your power, and where are the charges you have brought?"

Had he a pistol I believe he would have shot me dead. His ground was cut from under him. The man who destroyed his every hope stood before us all, and refuted his terrible charges. For a minute he stood as if irresolute; then he turned to Miss Forrest and spoke as coolly as if nothing had happened.

"May I claim your pardon, your forgiveness?" he said. "Believe me, lady, it was all because I loved you that I have acted as I have. Say, then, now that all is against me, that you forgive me."

She hesitated a minute before replying; then she said slowly, "It is difficult for me to speak to you without shuddering. Never did I believe such villainy possible; but—but I pray that God may forgive you, as I do."

"Then I will leave you," he said, with a terrible look at me.

"No," I said; "you will not leave us so easily. Know, man, that you are punishable by the law of England."

"How?"

"You are guilty of many things that I need not enumerate here; some Kaffar has told me about, some I knew before. So, instead of my lying in a felon's cell, it will be you."

Then we all received a great shock. Miss Staggles arose from her chair and rushed towards me.

"No, no, Mr. Blake," she cried; "no, not for my sake. He's my only son. For my sake, spare him."

"*Your* only son? *Yours?*" cried Miss Forrest's aunt.

"Mine," cried this gaunt old woman. "Oh, I was married on the Continent when quite a girl, and I dared not tell of it, for my husband was a gambler and a villain; but he was handsome and fascinating, and so he won me. Herod, this son of mine, was born just the day before his father was killed in a duel. Oh, spare him for my sake!"

I need not enter into the further explanations she made, nor how she pleaded for mercy for him, for they were painful to all. And did I spare him? Yes; on condition that he left England, never to return again, besides stipulating for Kaffar's safety.

He left the house soon after, and we all felt a sense of relief when he had gone, save Miss Staggles, or rather Mrs. Voltaire, who went up to her room weeping bitterly.

Need I relate what followed that night? Need I tell how I had to recount my doings and journeyings over again and again, while Simon and Kaffar were asked to give such information as I was unable to give, and how one circumstance was explained by another until all was plain? I will not tax my readers' patience by so doing; this must be left to their own imagination.

After this, Mrs. Walters insisted that we must have refreshments, and bustled away to order it, while a servant conducted Simon and Kaffar to a room where food was to be obtained; and so I was left alone with the woman I loved.

"Well?" I said, when they were gone.

"Well?" she replied, looking shyly into my face.

"I have done your bidding," I said, after a minute's silence. "I have freed you from that man."

"Thank God, you have!" she said, with a shudder. "Oh, if you only knew how I have prayed and hoped and thought!"

"And I had a promise, too," I said; "will it be painful for you to keep it?"

"Painful, Justin?" she cried. "You know I will gladly be your wife."

I will not write of what happened then. It is not for the eyes of the world to see. Tears come into my eyes now as I remember how her new-found happiness lit up her eyes with joy, and how the colour came into her beautiful cheeks. God alone knows how happy we were. We had been kept asunder by a cruel hand, and had been brought together again by long and bitter struggles, struggles which would never have been but for the love of God and the love in our hearts. Then, when our joy was fullest, a choir from a neighbouring church began to sing—

"Christians, awake, salute the happy morn, Whereon the Saviour of mankind was born."

It was indeed, a happy Christmas morn to us. The darkness had rolled away, and the light of heaven shone upon us.

When I left shortly after, I asked whether I should come the next day, or rather when daylight came, and spend Christmas Day with her.

"You must not be later than nine o'clock," she said, with a glad laugh, while my heart seemed ready to break for joy.

I have nearly told my story now; the loving work of months is almost at an end, and soon I must drop my pen. I am very happy, happier than I ever hoped to be. My new-found strength not only brought me freedom from my enemy, not only enabled me to accomplish my purpose, but gave me fuller and richer life. Gertrude and I live under brighter skies than we should do had I not been led through so terrible an experience. Thus the Eternal Goodness brings good out of evil.

Voltaire is on the Continent. I do not think that he has ever returned to England; while his mother, who still lives the same kind of life as of yore, supplies him with money. It appears that she has means which were unknown to her friends, and thus she keeps him supplied. Of course the relationship between them explains their being in league in Yorkshire. She was ever seeking to serve him then; she is still trying to do the same. She never speaks to me. But for me, she says, her son would have married Gertrude, and then she would have lived with her Herod, who would have been a country gentleman, not the poor outcast he is now.

Kaffar has gone back to Egypt. He stayed in London a few days after the scene on Christmas Eve, and I gave him house-room in my old lodgings; but he tired of England, so I sent him back to Cairo. I think he is a far better man than he was, but I am not at all sorry that he dislikes England. He writes sometimes, but I never receive his letters without thinking of the terrible night on the Yorkshire moors—of the dark waters, the red hand, and the terrible struggle. Although I am now entirely free from any such influences, I cannot help fearfully wondering at the awful power one being can exert over another. How an evil man could almost deplete me of my own self, and make me see according to his will and act according to his desires, is to me beyond explanation. Truly does our greatest poet say—

"We are such stuff
As dreams are made of, and our little life
Is rounded with a sleep."

Tom Temple is married, and lives happily at Temple Hall. Tom attributes all his happiness to the ghost. He should never have had the pluck to ask Edith Gray to be his wife, he says, had not his lady-love been so fearful.

"But you found no difficulty in getting her consent, Tom?" I said one day at Temple Hall.

"Difficulty!" laughed Tom. "She said 'Yes' before I had stuttered out my little speech."

"I couldn't bear to see you in such an agony of pain," blushingly replied his happy little wife.

Ah, well, Tom deserves his happiness, because he makes those around him happy.

Simon Slowden lives with Gertrude and me. He declared that he couldn't bear the idea of leaving us, after he'd gone through so much to bring us together. We are not sorry for this, for he has been an incalculable help to me in many ways. But for him, perhaps, I should never have the treasure I now possess, the truest and noblest wife God ever gave to man; but for him, I might have dragged out my weary life, disappointed and almost broken-hearted. Of course this might not be so; but I know that Simon was one of my greatest helpers in making me the happiest man on earth.

I will close my story with a secret. Yesterday, Simon came to me, looking very grave.

"If I remember aright, yer honour," he said, "I told you as 'ow I'd completely finished wi' all belongin' to the female persuasion."

"You did, Simon."

"Well, I've changed my mind. I used to think after that waccinatin' business gived me small-pox, that I was done for; but that 'ere Emily the 'ousemaid 'ev bin waccinated, and she 'ev had small-pox too. Well, 't seems to me as 'ow it must hev bin special Providence as hev brought us together, as we read in the Book of Job; and not likin' to go 'gin Providence, I axed her to change her name to Slowden."

"Well, Simon, what was her reply?"

Joseph Hocking

"She seed the force o' my reasonin's in a minute, and so, as you may say, 'there'll be good brought out o' evil,' even the evil o' waccinatin'; for it's give us both small-pox, and we both live. Our faces be a bit pitty, but kisses ain't none the less sweet for that."

"And when is it to come off, Simon?"

"I'm goin' to the registrar's now, yer honour, so three weeks to-morrow I shall be took in and done for, and all threw waccination."

THE END

Choose from Thousands of 1stWorldLibrary Classics By

A. M. Barnard	Booth Tarkington	Edward Everett Hale
Ada Leverson	Boyd Cable	Edward J. O'Biren
Adolphus William Ward	Bram Stoker	Edward S. Ellis
Aesop	C. Collodi	Edwin L. Arnold
Agatha Christie	C. E. Orr	Eleanor Atkins
Alexander Aaronsohn	C. M. Ingleby	Eleanor Hallowell Abbott
Alexander Kielland	Carolyn Wells	Eliot Gregory
Alexandre Dumas	Catherine Parr Traill	Elizabeth Gaskell
Alfred Gatty	Charles A. Eastman	Elizabeth McCracken
Alfred Ollivant	Charles Amory Beach	Elizabeth Von Arnim
Alice Duer Miller	Charles Dickens	Ellem Key
Alice Turner Curtis	Charles Dudley Warner	Emerson Hough
Alice Dunbar	Charles Farrar Browne	Emilie F. Carlen
Allen Chapman	Charles Ives	Emily Bronte
Alleyne Ireland	Charles Kingsley	Emily Dickinson
Ambrose Bierce	Charles Klein	Enid Bagnold
Amelia E. Barr	Charles Hanson Towne	Enilor Macartney Lane
Amory H. Bradford	Charles Lathrop Pack	Erasmus W. Jones
Andrew Lang	Charles Romyn Dake	Ernie Howard Pie
Andrew McFarland Davis	Charles Whibley	Ethel May Dell
Andy Adams	Charles Willing Beale	Ethel Turner
Angela Brazil	Charlotte M. Braeme	Ethel Watts Mumford
Anna Alice Chapin	Charlotte M. Yonge	Eugene Sue
Anna Sewell	Charlotte Perkins Stetson	Eugenie Foa
Annie Besant	Clair W. Hayes	Eugene Wood
Annie Hamilton Donnell	Clarence Day Jr.	Eustace Hale Ball
Annie Payson Call	Clarence E. Mulford	Evelyn Everett-green
Annie Roe Carr	Clemence Housman	Everard Cotes
Annonaymous	Confucius	F. H. Cheley
Anton Chekhov	Coningsby Dawson	F. J. Cross
Archibald Lee Fletcher	Cornelis DeWitt Wilcox	F. Marion Crawford
Arnold Bennett	Cyril Burleigh	Fannie E. Newberry
Arthur C. Benson	D. H. Lawrence	Federick Austin Ogg
Arthur Conan Doyle	Daniel Defoe	Ferdinand Ossendowski
Arthur M. Winfield	David Garnett	Fergus Hume
Arthur Ransome	Dinah Craik	Florence A. Kilpatrick
Arthur Schnitzler	Don Carlos Janes	Fremont B. Deering
Arthur Train	Donald Keyhoe	Francis Bacon
Atticus	Dorothy Kilner	Francis Darwin
B.H. Baden-Powell	Dougan Clark	Frances Hodgson Burnett
B. M. Bower	Douglas Fairbanks	Frances Parkinson Keyes
B. C. Chatterjee	E. Nesbit	Frank Gee Patchin
Baroness Emmuska Orczy	E. P. Roe	Frank Harris
Baroness Orczy	E. Phillips Oppenheim	Frank Jewett Mather
Basil King	E. S. Brooks	Frank L. Packard
Bayard Taylor	Earl Barnes	Frank V. Webster
Ben Macomber	Edgar Rice Burroughs	Frederic Stewart Isham
Bertha Muzzy Bower	Edith Van Dyne	Frederick Trevor Hill
Bjornstjerne Bjornson	Edith Wharton	Frederick Winslow Taylor

Friedrich Kerst
Friedrich Nietzsche
Fyodor Dostoyevsky
G.A. Henty
G.K. Chesterton
Gabrielle E. Jackson
Garrett P. Serviss
Gaston Leroux
George A. Warren
George Ade
Geroge Bernard Shaw
George Cary Eggleston
George Durston
George Ebers
George Eliot
George Gissing
George MacDonald
George Meredith
George Orwell
George Sylvester Viereck
George Tucker
George W. Cable
George Wharton James
Gertrude Atherton
Gordon Casserly
Grace E. King
Grace Gallatin
Grace Greenwood
Grant Allen
Guillermo A. Sherwell
Gulielma Zollinger
Gustav Flaubert
H. A. Cody
H. B. Irving
H.C. Bailey
H. G. Wells
H. H. Munro
H. Irving Hancock
H. R. Naylor
H. Rider Haggard
H. W. C. Davis
Haldeman Julius
Hall Caine
Hamilton Wright Mabie
Hans Christian Andersen
Harold Avery
Harold McGrath
Harriet Beecher Stowe
Harry Castlemon
Harry Coghill
Harry Houidini

Hayden Carruth
Helent Hunt Jackson
Helen Nicolay
Hendrik Conscience
Hendy David Thoreau
Henri Barbusse
Henrik Ibsen
Henry Adams
Henry Ford
Henry Frost
Henry James
Henry Jones Ford
Henry Seton Merriman
Henry W Longfellow
Herbert A. Giles
Herbert Carter
Herbert N. Casson
Herman Hesse
Hildegard G. Frey
Homer
Honore De Balzac
Horace B. Day
Horace Walpole
Horatio Alger Jr.
Howard Pyle
Howard R. Garis
Hugh Lofting
Hugh Walpole
Humphry Ward
Ian Maclaren
Inez Haynes Gillmore
Irving Bacheller
Isabel Cecilia Williams
Isabel Hornibrook
Israel Abrahams
Ivan Turgenev
J.G.Austin
J. Henri Fabre
J. M. Barrie
J. M. Walsh
J. Macdonald Oxley
J. R. Miller
J. S. Fletcher
J. S. Knowles
J. Storer Clouston
J. W. Duffield
Jack London
Jacob Abbott
James Allen
James Andrews
James Baldwin

James Branch Cabell
James DeMille
James Joyce
James Lane Allen
James Lane Allen
James Oliver Curwood
James Oppenheim
James Otis
James R. Driscoll
Jane Abbott
Jane Austen
Jane L. Stewart
Janet Aldridge
Jens Peter Jacobsen
Jerome K. Jerome
Jessie Graham Flower
John Buchan
John Burroughs
John Cournos
John F. Kennedy
John Gay
John Glasworthy
John Habberton
John Joy Bell
John Kendrick Bangs
John Milton
John Philip Sousa
John Taintor Foote
Jonas Lauritz Idemil Lie
Jonathan Swift
Joseph A. Altsheler
Joseph Carey
Joseph Conrad
Joseph E. Badger Jr
Joseph Hergesheimer
Joseph Jacobs
Jules Vernes
Julian Hawthrone
Julie A Lippmann
Justin Huntly McCarthy
Kakuzo Okakura
Karle Wilson Baker
Kate Chopin
Kenneth Grahame
Kenneth McGaffey
Kate Langley Bosher
Kate Langley Bosher
Katherine Cecil Thurston
Katherine Stokes
L. A. Abbot
L. T. Meade

L. Frank Baum
Latta Griswold
Laura Dent Crane
Laura Lee Hope
Laurence Housman
Lawrence Beasley
Leo Tolstoy
Leonid Andreyev
Lewis Carroll
Lewis Sperry Chafer
Lilian Bell
Lloyd Osbourne
Louis Hughes
Louis Joseph Vance
Louis Tracy
Louisa May Alcott
Lucy Fitch Perkins
Lucy Maud Montgomery
Luther Benson
Lydia Miller Middleton
Lyndon Orr
M. Corvus
M. H. Adams
Margaret E. Sangster
Margret Howth
Margaret Vandercook
Margaret W. Hungerford
Margret Penrose
Maria Edgeworth
Maria Thompson Daviess
Mariano Azuela
Marion Polk Angellotti
Mark Overton
Mark Twain
Mary Austin
Mary Catherine Crowley
Mary Cole
Mary Hastings Bradley
Mary Roberts Rinehart
Mary Rowlandson
M. Wollstonecraft Shelley
Maud Lindsay
Max Beerbohm
Myra Kelly
Nathaniel Hawthrone
Nicolo Machiavelli
O. F. Walton
Oscar Wilde

Owen Johnson
P.G. Wodehouse
Paul and Mabel Thorne
Paul G. Tomlinson
Paul Severing
Percy Brebner
Percy Keese Fitzhugh
Peter B. Kyne
Plato
Quincy Allen
R. Derby Holmes
R. L. Stevenson
R. S. Ball
Rabindranath Tagore
Rahul Alvares
Ralph Bonehill
Ralph Henry Barbour
Ralph Victor
Ralph Waldo Emmerson
Rene Descartes
Ray Cummings
Rex Beach
Rex E. Beach
Richard Harding Davis
Richard Jefferies
Richard Le Gallienne
Robert Barr
Robert Frost
Robert Gordon Anderson
Robert L. Drake
Robert Lansing
Robert Lynd
Robert Michael Ballantyne
Robert W. Chambers
Rosa Nouchette Carey
Rudyard Kipling
Saint Augustine
Samuel B. Allison
Samuel Hopkins Adams
Sarah Bernhardt
Sarah C. Hallowell
Selma Lagerlof
Sherwood Anderson
Sigmund Freud
Standish O'Grady
Stanley Weyman
Stella Benson
Stella M. Francis

Stephen Crane
Stewart Edward White
Stijn Streuvels
Swami Abhedananda
Swami Parmananda
T. S. Ackland
T. S. Arthur
The Princess Der Ling
Thomas A. Janvier
Thomas A Kempis
Thomas Anderton
Thomas Bailey Aldrich
Thomas Bulfinch
Thomas De Quincey
Thomas Dixon
Thomas H. Huxley
Thomas Hardy
Thomas More
Thornton W. Burgess
U. S. Grant
Upton Sinclair
Valentine Williams
Various Authors
Vaughan Kester
Victor Appleton
Victor G. Durham
Victoria Cross
Virginia Woolf
Wadsworth Camp
Walter Camp
Walter Scott
Washington Irving
Wilbur Lawton
Wilkie Collins
Willa Cather
Willard F. Baker
William Dean Howells
William le Queux
W. Makepeace Thackeray
William W. Walter
William Shakespeare
Winston Churchill
Yei Theodora Ozaki
Yogi Ramacharaka
Young E. Allison
Zane Grey